# AN INVITATION TO THOSE WHO LOVE RIVERS

## P.A. RAMACHANDRAN

The profits obtained from publishing this book will be utilized for the enhancement of environmental quality and pollution prevention initiatives in India.

INDIA · SINGAPORE · MALAYSIA

ISBN 979-8-88883-692-7

# AN INVITATION TO THOSE WHO LOVE RIVERS

(A former Ganga Action Plan engineer's narrative on the features and lesser known peculiarities including the pollution control activities of some Indian as well as foreign rivers, thus providing an interesting study in contrast for river lovers.)

I dedicate this book to late Professor M.K. Prasad, the former Pro-Vice-Chancellor of Calicut University, and the leader of the science movement 'Kerala Sastra Sahitya Parishath'. Prof. Prasad, known for his untiring grass root level efforts to protect our rivers and tropical rain forests till he fell to Covid 19 in the year 2022, was also a very popular Indian environmental activist who led the historical 'Save Silent Valley' agitation of the 1970s.

# About the Author

**P.A. Ramachandran**

Mr. P.A. Ramachandran from Panikkan parambil Houe, Kattoor village, Thrissur, Kerala, is an engineer by profession. A graduate in Civil Engineering from the College of Engineering, Trivandrum, he did his post-graduations from the Indian Institute of Hygiene & Public Health (Kolkata) and the California State University, USA. Mr. Ramachandran was also a Fellow of the World Health Organization (WHO) during 1980-1981.

Mr. Ramachandran started his career as an Engineer with the Kerala State PWD. Later he shifted to Kerala Water Authority (then known as Public Health Engineering Department), and then to the Kerala State Pollution Control Board as its Regional Engineer, Calicut. He has also worked as the Registrar of CWRDM, as a Consultant for Ganga Action Plan, as the Head of the Environment & Safety Dept, govt. of Dubai, as the Senior Controller of Pollution in the Ministry of Environment, Oman, and finally as a Lead Auditor for TUV-NORD, Germany. His core expertise is in the preparation of Environment Management Systems for industrial and development projects.

It was Mr. Ramachandran, who, as the Head of the Environment and Safety Departments of Dubai Municipality in its formative years, pioneered the environmental and safety planning activities of the Emirates. Later, during his days as the Senior Controller of Pollution with the Oman Government, Mr. Ramachandran helped in laying down the rules for the import of chemicals to the sultanate, prescribing quality standards for recycled water, and controlling hazardous wastes besides his regular pollution control duties there.

During his days with the Pollution Control Board, Kerala, Mr. Ramachandran was instrumental in initiating legal procedures for eliminating the pollution problems in the Chaliyar River basin and Bharatha Puzha. As a consultant with the Ganga Action Plan, he played a key role in the installation of effluent treatment plants in the textile mills of the National Textile Corporation and the tanneries in the Kanpur industrial belt, the biggest pollutants of river Ganga till then. His contributions to the academic field include teaching 'Disaster Management' in the Muscat off campus of Caledonian Engineering college, UK, and conducting short term package courses on quality, environment, energy, occupational safety and food safety management system as per the relevant ISO standards. Mr. Ramachandran had been to more than two dozen countries for training, system audits and related activities.

Mr. Ramachandran is the author of the Malayalam books 'Ee Kalavum Kadannu Pokum', 'Nakshatrangale thottu Nilkumbol', and 'Ente Haritha Yatrakal'.

Wife: Dr. Leena Devi. Daughter: Dr. Anupama Kothari.
Grandchildren: Aandhara and Agastya.
Mobile No: +918433750670.  Email: lahse1972@gmail.com

# About The Translator

Mr. Kurian Thomas, the translator of this book is a college-mate of the author Mr. P.A. Ramachandran. He was a Superintending Engineer (Mechanical) of the State-owned  Oil and Natural Gas Corporation; and later, a Vice President (Quality Control & Inspection) with FL Smidth, Denmark when he finally retired.

# Introduction

## K. Jayakumar, IAS (Former Chief Secretary)

Those who love rivers are those who love life; those who love mother earth. They are capable of appreciating life and its beauty in its entirety through all situations. That's the discernment of their mind. They don't have to be poets, painters, or recognized artists. Their education and calling may be mathematics or engineering. Still, they are blessed with a heart which can assimilate nature's love and wonders.

Mr. P.A. Ramachandran is an environmental engineer by karma. There is only one explanation for Ramachandran's obsession with rivers. This book "An Invitation to Those Who Love Rivers along the Shores of the Great Cultures' with no parallels, is the soliloquy of that man whose passion is communing with rivers. In his reflections, there are so many details like rivers' connection with mythology, history of civilizations as well as art forms like literature, sculpture and dance blooming on river banks; and above all, there is an intriguing curiosity to know the biological identity of rivers. Books on a single river (especially the River Ganga) may be rare in Malayalam; but not so in English. However, other than this book, I haven't seen any work in Malayalam or English with a comprehensive understanding of eighteen rivers. The author's insistence on portraying how each of these eighteen rivers differs from all others, makes this book extremely readable. This work is woven with knowledge and emotion as warp and weft.

Here's a portion from the chapter 'Cauvery' in this book disclosing its character:

"There is yet another reason for Thanjavoor and Kaveri attracting world attention. Tiruvaiyaru, the venue of the world-famous annual Thyagaraja music festival is in the Thanjavur district. Maybe because of this, Kaveri appears to be moving rather slowly in this stretch. Can't blame her because, who will be in a hurry to leave the place echoing the religious music and song 'Jagadananda karaka' in 'natta raga', and 'Enthro Mahanubhavalu', the fifth song in 'sri raga'?"

Similarly, in the chapter on River Godavari, the author summarizes the relationship between River Godavari and Ramayana with utmost moderation. "It was in the Dandakam forests on the banks of River Godavari that some of the most critical events of the epic Ramayana took place. Events like Soorpanakha's misdemeanours to entice Lord Sri Rama provoking Laxman to chop off her nose and boobs apart, Lord Rama killing the Kharabhooshans, Mareechan the illusionist disguised as the golden deer fooling Sita devi to come out of the safe confines of the 'Laxman Rekha', Ravana kidnapping Sitadevi as she breached the 'Laxman Rekha' etc, were staged in the Dandakam forests."

As per the Indian culture, rivers, mountains, plants, animals, soil, wind and fire are believed to have an element of divinity in them inherently. That's neither a superstition nor amorality. It is faith. Man, who is created out of Panchabhootha, the five elements earth, sky, air, fire and water is obliged to treat them as divine; and protect them. They're the ones who sustain us, and keep us going. They deserve respect and humility from us. That is the only intention of bestowing that concept of holiness on them. But, in today's ungrateful world where man has given the go-by to all such values, and has transformed as Bhasmasura who raised his hand to immolate none other than Lord Siva who gave him that boon, this book has taken upon itself a great moral mission by focusing on the role of rivers in sustaining life. This book taking the readers for a trek through the river banks will leave them spellbound by the details in it, and delight them with its narrative brilliance; but at the same time the descriptions in it on the kind of pollution these rivers are being subjected to, will leave them heart-broken. It is the river which gives us everything starting with our very life. But, what are we giving back to them. This book raises many unpleasant questions which we have always hesitated to ask ourselves. This informative and emotionally rich work on the rivers will not fail to shake our conscience, and shed our apathy.

From all over the world, we hear stories of disputes over the sharing of the water in the rivers that flow through multiple countries and even through states within a country. Our rivers including Sindhu, Kaveri, Brahmaputra and Krishna too are not free from this curse. This author, who believes that water, the gift of nature belongs equally to all, can look only sadly at the endless disputes between the Indian states over river water sharing. It is only natural for the writer, who is also an environmental engineer who worked in Ganga Action Plan, to throw his weight behind the idea of river interlinking as a solution to such disputes. But it remains to be seen whether human beings will be as generous as rivers to accommodate everyone's interests so long as the river water remains as an issue of emotional and political significance.

Civilization was born on the banks of the rivers. That civilization further progressed through industrial revolution propelled by scientific advancements. It is a historical paradox that industries, which are the products of civilization nurtured by rivers, are today the biggest polluters of those very same rivers. As a result, there is no river in India which is not choking from industrial pollution. Even the sacred river Ganga which was supposed to have the ability to self-purify, is overwhelmed by pollution to gain notoriety as one of the most polluted rivers in the world today. The efficacy of governmental initiatives to address river pollution like the 'Namami Gange' project is only marginal compared to the scale of the problem. River pollution is not something that can be resolved by governmental interference alone. The entire country has to become vigilant about it. There are stories of rivers like the Thames and the Rhine in Europe to have gained salvation from this scourge when those nations realized the consequences of the problem and rose in unison to address it. People should forget their political and sectarian affiliations, and come together to create a social and political environment conducive to reach the goal. Divided societies will lose the will power to protect rivers, the unique gifts of nature, the author laments.

The readers of this book will inevitably realize one eternal truth. The reality of how inseparably and emotionally are rivers intertwined with our lives. A truth that many of us have forgotten in the torrent of today's fast, materialistic life. Is there anyone in India who hasn't heard of the great stories about River Ganga? Aren't we associated with Ganga, Yamuna, Brahmaputra and Cauvery by instinct; and not by religious or parochial considerations? Aren't the culture and heritage that we are proud of, gifts from these rivers? Just think of the great temples which came up on river banks, the festivals and rituals like the Mahakumbha melas that have developed around those temples, the pilgrimages, even the floating aaratis. These rivers flow through our lives giving us so many cultural diversities; the same way, they flowed through the lives of our ancestors, and will continue to do so to enrich the lives of our future generations as well.

Ramachandran writes: "Ganges is not just a river; she is the emotion of the whole nation. It is not water that flows through it. Rather, they are the elements of the great culture that sustains the Indian people. Flourishing on its shores is the great heritage of thousands of years. This book will spawn a new love affair between the readers and rivers, I am sure.

In this book, Mr. Ramachandran is not limiting his disclosures to Indian rivers. There are many interesting revelations and anecdotes about the rivers he visited namely Rhine River in Germany, the St. Lawrence River in Canada, the Thames River in Britain, Potomac and Sacramento rivers in US, and the Jordan River in the Middle East providing a highly enlightening study in contrast, especially on the vexed issue of controlling pollution in rivers.

# Contents

# Preface

"The next war in our region will be fought over water, not politics." These were the words of Mr. Boutros Boutros-Ghali when he was a minister with the government of Egypt. Mr. Boutros-Ghali later on became the Secretary-General of the United Nations.

When Mr. Boutros-Ghali made that statement in 1985, very few people took it seriously. But today, not only in that region, the world over, river water disputes are among the major reasons for the squabbles and skirmishes between even communities, thus more than validating the prophecy of Mr. Boutros-Ghali.

Various Indian civilizations had their origins in the river valleys. For us, rivers are much more than just carriers of water. It is on their banks that human settlements sprouted. Our rich cultural heritage blossomed drawing from the stimulating environs of the shores and banks of our rivers.

What Ganga, Sindhu, Kaveri and their lesser known sisters gave us was much more than just means of livelihood. They provided the most inspiring ambience for the formation and development of languages, literature, music, and everything else we see in our lives today.

It is our rivers which earned for India a place of pride in the annals of the cultural evolution of the world. While our Indus Valley civilisation of around 2000 BC or older and the Ganges Valley civilisation of the Vedic period dating back to around of 1500 BC were the earliest cradles of civilisation in the North, that credit goes to rivers Kaveri and Vaigai in the South; with both providing the perfect settings for the growth of a civilisation of its own heritage. It is from the hermitages along the banks of our rivers that the ancient world's seats of learning like Nalanda, Taxshila, Kanchi, Vikramashila etc got enriched. What we are today, is because of these rivers.

All our great epics took birth in the backdrop of the river valleys. Sage Valkimi, the Aadi Kavi wrote the first epic poem Ramayanam sitting in his hermitage on the banks of Tamassa river, a tributary of Ganges. Down South, the Chilappathikaram, the evergreen story of Kannaki, the embodiment of Tamil pride was born on the banks of Kaveri. Rivers always fuelled the imagination and inspired creativity.

I don't remember when exactly my love affair with the rivers started. Born at Kattoor near Irinjalakkuda, I didn't have much interaction with rivers in my childhood. As a person who was heaved into the sea of near destitution after having lost both my parents by the age of twenty, perhaps, my professional involvement with the rivers provided me with the much needed solace, and that led to the creation of the bond between me and the rivers. As an Environment Engineer, I had the good fortune of participating in the cleansing of many rivers in India and abroad. In my job as the very first Regional Engineer of the Kerala State Pollution Control Board at Kozhikode in the 1980s, it was I who monitored, planned and set rolling the anti-pollution activities in the rivers in North Kerala for the first time, and that paved the way for a lifelong, inseparable bond between me and the rivers. It was my commitment to the rivers which energised me in taking a firm, uncompromising stand against the Gwalior Rayons factory at Mavoor, Kozhikode - discharges from where were polluting the Chaliyar River most - despite opposition to my efforts from even the powers that mattered, as well as the non-cooperation of some colleagues.

I love travelling. I have travelled a lot in India and abroad during my four decades long official life. My foot-falls are there on almost all continents. Wherever I went, my first interest was in knowing as much as I could about the rivers there. On such trips, I also found time to visit them amidst my busy schedules. In India, I had the good fortune of seeing most of our rivers. Needless to say, my official engagement with the Ganga Action Plan facilitated my interaction with the rivers extensive and authentic. And now, destiny has bestowed on me this opportunity of presenting all those memories in this book form.

But, that is not to suggest that all my informations about rivers are positive. The sad part about our rivers is that, among all the rivers in the world, Indian rivers are among the most polluted. To give you a basic idea of the gravity of the problem, the CPCB (Central Pollution Control Board) has divided the river waters into five categories as A, B, C, D, and E on the basis of quality. Category A is the top-most ranking one, and that water is supposed to be potable – of course after minimal purifications like filtration and clorination. The technical requirement of this grade of river water is that, it should contain at least 6 mg of dissolved oxygen. The BOD (Biochemical Oxygen Demand) which is the yardstick for organic impurities shouldn't exceed 2 BOD. Similarly, the pH value should be between 6.5 and 8. The bacteria count also shouldn't exceed 50 MFN in 100 ml of water. Many rivers in Europe and Scandinavian countries boast of holding water of grade 'A'.

Category 'B' water is the one which is considered fit for taking bath. The quality requirements are not as stringent as that of Category 'A'.

Category 'C' river water is still more tolerant to impurities. For example, among other things, it allows the MFN limit upto 5000/ 100 ml. This grade of water as well as category 'B' water could be stored in the reservoiers and distributed as potable water after purification and treatment to bring their quality to that of category 'A'.

Next is, category D. The specifications for this grade is much more liberal. This water is considered fit for aquaculture and related activities only.

The last grade is category 'E'. The requirement for a river water to qualify as category 'E' are atrocious to say the least. This water is not recommended for any purposes,

Unfortunately, the river water in some stretches of many of our rivers is so bad that, they won't qualify to be categorised even as 'E'.

To understand the seriousness of this problem, when a river gets polluted, that will have a cascading effect not only along its flow, but also in the land mass as the polluted water percolates into the land mass on either sides. Thus, that pollution fouls up the springs and wells at places even far away. That is what I could see on the people as well as the flora and fauna in the villages near the Chaliyar river during the period when the pollution in that river was at its peak.

Pollution apart, the water situation in India is dire. In the 75 years since Independence, the annual per capita availability of water has declined by 75% - from 6,000 cubic meters in 1947 to 1,500 cubic meters in 2021. This is due to not only of the increase in population, but also, to the depletion in groundwater, pollution of surface water; and the vanishing of water bodies - ponds, lakes, tanks, wetlands etc, due to encroachments. In some States like Punjab, the ground water extraction is much higher than the safe limit of under 70% resulting in the lowering of the water table year after year. This can't be sustained, and unless checked soon, will have far reaching consequences. By fooling around with water, we are actually 'playing with fire'. This book is intended to convey this message to the esteemed readers.

We humans can draw a very valuable lesson from the life of the rivers. Please listen to the words of the famous Lebanese poet Khalil Gibran. According to him, a river originating mostly from a mountain, flows frolicking happily through waterfalls, valleys, countryside believing that this is the way her life will be all through. But, suddenly she awakes to the reality as she reaches the estuary awaiting to merge her with the sea. She shivers with fear, as she sees in front of her a vast ocean ready to swallow her. But there is no other way. She cannot flow back.

So, the river enters the ocean resigned to her fate. But, once she enters the ocean, she realises that she was not disappearing into the ocean, but becoming the ocean. What seemed like the end of her life was in reality an act of merging back with from where she originated because, every drop in a river had come from the oceans. So, don't be scared when death knocks at your door because you are only about to merge your identity with the supreme source. This is the lesson we all can draw from the life of rivers.

In sustaining life on this planet, the importance of rivers is next only to the air we breathe. Each river is a carrier of the nectar of life. Rivers are the arteries of mother earth. If we are able to convey this message to the next generation, that will outweigh all the physical assets we earn and leave for them. When we mindlessly exploit nature for our selfish interests, what we are actually doing is, leaving the planet difficult to live for the future generations who will be cursed to put up with never ending cycles of pandemics, and cheated of much of the plant and animal lives we see around today. Fortunately for them, though a bit belatedly, the government has come alive to the threats, and have initiated schemes like 'Ini Njan Ozhukatte' (Let Me Flow Now), 'Punarjeni' (Rebirth), the novel concept "forestry interventions" briefed in the chapter 'Ganga' etc aimed at rejuvenating our rivers.

In this book, I have tried to include whatever information I could gather about rivers during my half a century long quest. Among them are many interesting historical and cultural details as well as folklores on the rivers lesser known to the present generation.

I respectfully present this book on the rivers of India to my readers who wholeheartedly received my other publications 'Reminiscences', "Reaching out to the Stars', 'Chaliyar' etc.

With love,
– P.A. Ramachandran,
Ph: 91 8433750670.

# SARASWATHI
## Divine But Invisible

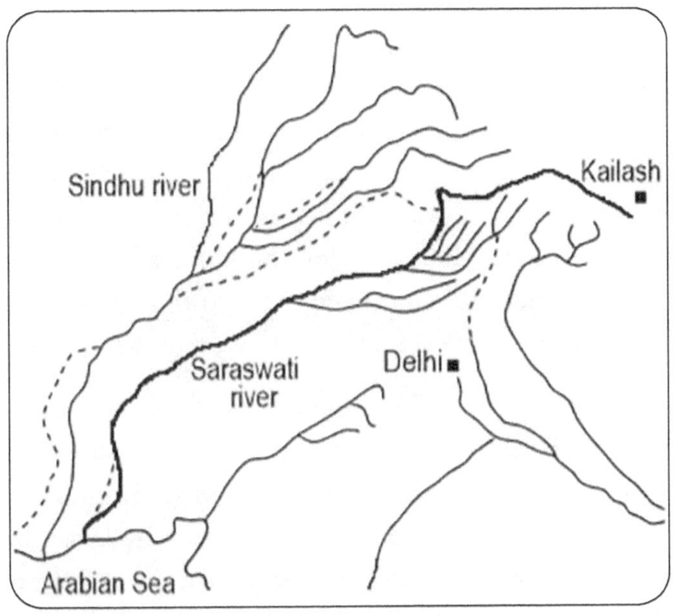

**Saraswathi River**

As per our tradition, paying obeisance to Saraswati, the goddess of 'letters' is the first thing we do as we take a writing instrument in hand. Here, that assumes added significance because I am starting this book writing about none other than Saraswati, the river. So, with the blessings of goddess Saraswati, let me begin.

Yes, as per Indian mythology, there are two Saraswatis; goddess Saraswati and the holy river Saraswati. Their similarity doesn't end with the name. Both are invisible too. River Saraswati is a mythical river flowing through the minds of the people, generation to generation.

Saraswati, the Goddess of letters, and Saraswathi, the holy river are supposed to be the two incarnations of the same divine power, alternating in those roles from time to time. The 'Srishti Kaandam' of the 'Padma Puranam' describes how Goddess Saraswathi became a river.

That story goes like this. For some reason, one day, sage Aurvan of 'Brigu' lineage got so angry as to threaten to burn down the whole world with his fiery temper. This forced Indra and the other Gods to run to Mahavishnu and request his help. What Vishnu did was, he collected the raging red-hot anger of the sage in a golden pot, and handed it over to goddess Saraswati with an instruction to immerse it in the Arabian Sea. Since it was impossible to go all the way till the Arabian sea carrying the red hot pot, what goddess Saraswati did was to transform herself into a river, flow down from 'Brahmalok' traversing the Himalayas, flow further west to reach 'Pushkara theertha'; and from there to the Arabian sea to merge with it along with the pot. A story difficult to swallow?

But, think twice before rubbishing off the stories of existence of river Saraswati as one of those folklores. Because, you can see river Saraswati finding mention along with rivers Ganga, Yamuna, Sindhu, Godavari etc in Mahabharatha. If Ganga, Yamuna, Sindhu and Godavari are real, that give credence to the argument that a river by name Saraswati existed here at one time. The reference to Saraswati River in Mahabharatha was not just a passing one. Many critical events in Mahabharatha lie entwined with Saraswati River. One is, Kurukshethra, the battle-field in the Mahabharatha war, was the plains between river Saraswati and river Rishadwati. Next, in the 'Vanapurvom' of Mahabharatha, it is mentioned that river Saraswati is one of the seven tributaries of river Ganga, and it is originating from 'Plava', a divine tree. Yet again, in chapter 36 of 'Vanapurvom', it is mentioned that 'Kamyaka Vanam' where the Pandavas lived for a long time during their anonymous life while in exile, was on the banks of Saraswati River; and in chapter 130, it says that river Saraswati disappears into the earth at

'Vinasa Theertha' and re-emerges at 'Chamasothbhetha'. All these point to the strong possibility that a river by name Saraswati existed here. Some people believe that the holy place known as Keshav Prayag is the place where river Saraswati meets river Alakananda. But, whatever be the truth, today, she has disappeared from the memories of most of us also.

In the past, on and off, sensational stories from here and there on finding the long lost river Saraswati used to get front page coverage in the newspapers. One of them was a news item titled "Rebirth of the Saraswati River which disappeared 4000 years back" from the Mugalvalley Village in Yamuna Nagar, Haryana. It all started with the Haryana Government's 'River Retrieval' scheme, under which, efforts were on to find river Saraswati. There, they dug up the area where the river was believed to have vanished, and met with a powerful gush of water. Encouraged with this finding, they continued with more digging believing that what they found was a part of river Saraswati; but, hasn't heard anything more about it afterwards. Elsewhere, some 3km from Badrinath, there is a place called 'Mana' where we can see a fountain gushing down from a cluster of boulders. Some swear that this is river Saraswati, but there is no official confirmation for it yet. Also, there is no trace of the upstream part of this flow.

Efforts to unravel the mystery behind this river in a more scientific way, were also made by the historians and archaeologists. Their conclusion is that, the river Saraswati was a reality; but, it either got merged with river Yamuna nearby, or got absorbed by the 'Thar' dessert following a huge earthquake some 4000 years ago. In the meantime, an expert committee appointed by the central government has reported that there are strong reasons to believe that river Saraswati is not a myth. In the opinion of Prof. K.S. Vaidya, the head of the panel which made this report, river Saraswati was a 4000 km long river which originated from the Himalayas, flowed through Haryana, Rajasthan, Northern Gujarat and Ran of Kutch in Pakistan before joining the Arabian sea. Another finding of this seven member Committee is that, river Saraswathi had two tributaries; with the western tributary having river Sutlej as a part of it. Also, it was at a place called Satrana, some 25 km south of Patiala where these tributaries met before entering Ran of Kutch; and the river was upto 5 km wide at some places. Lending credence to these revelations, it is heard that ISRO's Remote Sensing Centre at Jodhpur has made some headway in locating the track of the Saraswati River.

I am nobody to say whether river Saraswati is a myth or a fact; though I had the good fortune of getting religiously acquainted with many rivers of India in course of my work, as well as during my private exploration trips. In the long list of my 'river friends' are Sindhu, Ganga, Yamuna, Kaveri, Krishna, Godavari, Perar, Periyar to mention a few. I am sure, being so committed and involved with the rivers, I have a right for an appointment with river Saraswati too; and hopefully, it won't be too long before it materialises. Till then, I will remain in the cool comfort stemming from my imagination that the holy river, with its rich cultural tradition of millions of years, is flowing majestically through my mind.

Let us hope, no other river meets with the fate of river Saraswati. May, all the rivers continue to flow for ever in all their majesty to enable mother earth wrap herself up in lush greenery till eternity, and support all forms of life in the planet.

We may have to wait a while more to retrieve river Saraswati; but, let us waste no time in retrieving the rivers of love and compassion, this generation seems to have lost somewhere along.

# SINDHU
## Cradle of Indian Civilization

**Indus River**

*"I beg for the forgiveness of the sins - if any - my beloved father might have committed, knowingly or unknowingly, during his time on this earth; and for the eternal salvation of his soul."*

"For that, I dip in Ganga, who has the power to wash away the sins,… and in Sindhu, the holy river."

That was the ritualistic prayer sputtered by me during the customary ash immersion - the last rites of my late father - being performed by me while dipping myself three times not in Ganga; but, in the chest deep water of a stream near my house. In my early twenties then, I was simply repeating these words recited to me by an aged temple priest in his broken words. I was so overwhelmed by the sombreness of that occasion that the tiny ripples in that small stream manifested in my mind as the waves of Ganga and Sindhu.

As I was immersing the ashes of my father in that stream chanting that prayer, I had taken an oath that I will visit all the holy rivers in India and perform the rites for the salvation and eternal peace of my parents as per Indian tradition. I could fulfil most of it within my mid-life. However, River Sindhu remained a mirage.

River Sindhu, with its own unique charm, has a prominent place in the Indian epics. In the Valmiki Ramayanam, there is a story about the birth of river Sindhu. It goes like this. King Bhageerath became ascetic and prayed to God for years on end enduring all kinds of hardships till the fulfilment of his desire to bring to earth River Ganga which was then flowing in the heaven. On the earth, it was at a place called Bindu Sarass below Mountain Kailassam where Ganga touched down. From there, it branched out as six distributaries. Three of them, Hladini, Pavani and Nalini flowed towards east, and the other three – Suchakshus, Sita and Sindhu flowed towards west.

River Sindhu finds mention in the Rigveda also. In the Mahabharatha, there is reference to a kingdom called Sindhu or Saindhavam. Dussala, the only sister of the Kauravas was married to Jayadradhan, the king of Sindhu. That apart, epics mention about kingdoms by name Sindhudweepam, Sindhu Pulindam, Sindhu Sauveeram etc on the bank of this great river. Sindhu also has a place as a holy river on par with Ganga in the hearts of many.

Myths and folklores apart, river Sindhu has played decisive roles in the history, culture and development of Noth-west India and Pakistan. This river, originating from Manasa Saras near Kailasam in the Himalayan Mountain Ranges, together with its tributaries meet most of the water needs of the farmers, as well as the industry there. River Sindhu, flowing west, is the only Himalayan River ending up in the Arabian sea. Traversing Jammu-Kashmir, Himachal Pradesh, Punjab, Rajastan and Haryana, and some provinces in Pakistan, the 3180 km long Sindhu also has the distinction as the longest river in the Indian sub-continent. If you consider the length of its tributaries also, that will add up to around 6000 km. Beas, Sutlej, Rabi (in India), Chinab, Jhelum (in Pakistan) are the five tributaries of River Sindhu.

It is in River Beas, also known as 'Vipasha' in the scriptures that the tourist spot Palani waterfalls is located. Beas River can also boast of the Pong dam, also known as Beas Dam alias Maharana Pratap Sagar Dam. Another dam in the Beas River is the Larji Dam. Renjit Sagar Dam, known also as Thein Dam is in River Rabi. It is in Sindhu's Indian tributary Sutlej that the 518.25 meters long Bhakra Nangal dam on the Punjab – Himachal border is built. At 207.26 m height, this is the tallest gravity dam in India. In Sindhu's Pakistan tributary Chinab, there are three hydro-electric projects by name Baglihar, Dulhasti and Salal. India and Pakistan are fighting a case in the International Court over some disputes on the Baglihar dam.

The biggest dam in this river is the Tarbala Dam, in Pakistan. On the 19th of September 1960, India and Pakistan signed the Sindhu Water Treaty. This treaty was brokered by the World Bank, and it was Prime Minister Nehru and President Ayub Khan respectively who signed for these two countries. As per this treaty, India has only 20% claim to Sindhu water.

The fact is, river water disputes between India and Pakistan has been an 'on – off' affair since long; and inevitably River Sindhu is at the centre of it all. The situation got worsened with the Uri conflict of 2016. There, the firing lasted some 6 hours. 17 Indian soldiers fell to Pakistani bullets. Many more were injured. Four Pakistani suicide attackers also lost their lives. Naturally, the conflict had its ripples in the diplomatic field also. India boycotted the SAARC Summit held at Islamabad in November 2016. Pakistan retaliated by blocking Indian television channels. Indian film producers entered the fray by banning Pakistani actors and artists.

Indian Cricket Control Board broke its ties with their Pakistani counterpart. India also requested ICC to avoid India playing Pakistan in the group matches of any tournament. In short, the Uri incident snowballed into spoiling India – Pakistan relationship in not only diplomatic; but, also social, political, cultural and sports fields. Indian Prime Minister assured the nation that India will give a fitting reply to Pakistan's misadventure, and the retaliatory measures will extend to India taking an uncompromising stand on Sindhu waters, adding that this will be a war with water to strip Pakistan of all its strength.

The biggest city on the banks of Sindhu is Karachi in Pakistan. Lahore is the biggest town on the banks of the tributary Rabi. The tombs of Jahangir and Noor Jahan are also on the banks of Rabi, at Shahdara Bagh (in Pakistan). Further on the tributaries of River Sindhu, it is on the banks of Jhelum that the Battle of Hydaspes between Emperor Alexander the Great and king Porus was fought in BC 326.

Another interesting fact about Sindhu is that, it is one of the only two Indian rivers – the other one being the Hubli river near Calcutta – where 'Tidal Bore', the rare tidal phenomenon of sea water rushing into the river to push the river back against the current, is experienced. May be, this is the reason why river Sindhu is described as an ocean in many of our epics.

My 'love affair' with Sindhu dates back to my school days. My desire to meet her in person stemmed from the information gathered from the school text books on Indus Valley Civilisation. Historians believe, it was around some 5000 years back that, people leading a nomadic life till then, began to settle down at one place, stay in the houses, organise farming, and live to the discipline of the community. Indus Valley Civilisation on the banks of River Sindhu is one among the earliest orderly human settlements discovered so far.

The discovery of the remnants of the Indus Valley Civilisation was quite accidental. In the year 1850, as the then British government was digging up earth for building a road from Lahore to Multan, they chanced upon some bricks. Pursuing that lead, explorers unearthed a huge treasure of an ancient civilisation now known as Mohenjodaro and Harappa in the Punjab and Sind provinces of Pakistan. There, the explorers were surprised at finding roads with drainage facilities; and houses with toilets, pipelines etc.

Enthused by all these information, I yearned to visit Islamabad, Lahore and Sindh, and see those left overs of that earliest civilisation. I had some chances too to fulfil that desire. Two of my colleagues in the Department of Environment of the Govt. of Dubai in the 1980s were Pakistanis – Mr. Amjad Khan and the six and a half feet tall Mr. Tariq. More than just colleagues, we were good friends; and they used to invite me to visit Pakistan every time I mentioned something about Pakistan. But, for one reason or the other, it didn't materialise. Years later, on a couple of occasions, I had even made preparations for it on my own. However, unexpected work pressures played spoil-sport forcing last moment cancellations. In the later years, the skirmishes between India and Pakistan created situations not exactly conducive for leisure trips to Pakistan, and I had to put the Sindhu visit in the backburner.

But, who can stop destiny? A long time ago, I had opened my mind about this disappointment to my friend Mr. Unni Bhaskar. Unni is the nephew of my classmate and friend Mr. C. K. Prabhakaran Nair. He is the MD and CEO of a company constructing control towers for the airports in India and the Gulf countries. Incidentally, I happened to be the Environment Auditor of that company.

Unni's organising skill is phenomenal. He has the knack for getting even the toughest of the tasks done quite effortlessly. So, not surprisingly, Unni is occupying many key positions in public institutions including some associated with the Sri Padmanabha Swamy Temple at Tiruvananthapuram. With Unni on my side, I never hesitated to plunge head on into any venture. We have travelled together in India and abroad many times. We have even undertaken some adventure trips like deep sea diving also.

Unni called me up one day in 2011 when we both were working in Muscat: "Uncle, do you still nurse your desire to visit River Sindhu you sounded me some time back? I spoke to my friend Mr. Dasaradhi, Group Captain of the Indian Air Force at Delhi. Now, there are no restrictions in people visiting Ladak and Punjab areas including the place where River Sindhu originates. If you want, you can use this trip to visit Jalianwala Bagh and the Golden Temple at Amritsar also. If it is okay with you, we can go there a week after Diwali."

I couldn't believe my ears. I am at the doorsteps of fulfilling a wish which I thought would never materialise. But, there was a catch. That was the time when the river water dispute between India and Pakistan was simmering. Going into a conflict area has got its own challenges. Situation can change within minutes without any forewarnings. What if I get stranded somewhere in that godforsaken mountain region? I am a person with many major illnesses; and was under strict medical advice to minimise travels, and never travel unless accompanied by a person capable of dealing with exigencies, if at all a travel becomes unavoidable. By and large, I was able to adhere to this instruction ever since. But, as I said earlier, I have no fear to go anywhere if Mr. Unni Bhaskar is there for company.

I replied to Unni "Yes, done".

We reached Delhi via Bombay. Group Captain Dasaradhi was living in the Defence Colony, Delhi. He was supposed to join us. That day, Delhi was blanketed in fog precipitated by air pollution, and that had led to the cancellation of many flights. We were in tenterhooks. Will our efforts go waste? For me, it is now or never. From our hotel room, we telephoned the airport. They told us that the weather is expected to clear within three hours. That provided little comfort because weather anywhere can play truant, and is infamous for letting you down at the least expected time. However, luckily for us, this time it was different. Group Captain Dasarathi reached the airport in time. The flight took off as scheduled, and we landed at Amritsar.

Amritsar, the biggest Indian city on the banks of Sindhu is where the Golden Temple of the Sikh community is located. We decided to go there first. This temple is in the middle of a pond, and there is a bridge to reach there. Naturally, there are restrictions on the entry of people there. We had to wait in a queue for nearly 2 hours for our turn to come. By the time we came out, it was noon. The organisers persuaded us to join in the 'Langar' there. It is a custom in all the Sikh temples that whoever is present there during the food timings, will be fed – no matter religion.

We too joined the Langar. That was one of the best lunches I ever had. That prompted me to request a volunteer whether I can have a look at their kitchen. He had no problems in obliging; and I followed him to the kitchen, leaving Unni Bhaskar and the Group Captain to have a look at a book stall and display windows. What I saw there was not a conventional kitchen filled with smoke; but, a huge factory where all the food items are prepared by machines. No wonder, the Sardars are known as a highly enterprising community, the world over. I salute them for everything that I saw and experienced during my visit to the Golden Temple.

Next in our itinerary was the visit to Jalianwala Baug, the arena where hundreds of freedom fighters were massacred in the year 1919. That day was April 13, the Baisakhi festival day. Baisakhi is the biggest 'Harvest Festival' in India. That is the first day of the Baisakh month which is the first month in the solar calendar of Punjabis. A big day for the Sikhs. Incidentally, it was on this day in the year 1699 that the Sikhs assumed their identity as a separate community.

On April 13 1919, the Indian National Congress which was spearheading the freedom struggle, had organised a public meeting at the Jalianwala Baug grounds. There are different stories on what for the meeting was called. One is, that was to protest the arrests of independence struggle leaders Dr. Saifuddin Kichlew and Dr. Satya Pal. Once the meeting started, a British Army Officer, Brigadier R.E.H. Dyer, with his army units surrounded the protesters, and started shooting at the crowd indiscriminately without any warning. Jalianwala Baug is a rectangular arena. With three of its sides fully closed by buildings, and the fourth side also having some structures, the Jalianwala Bagh ground had only one narrow exit. The firing was after blocking it, and it lasted till the ammunition got exhausted. Many people fell to the bullets. That apart, the trapped protesters who ran helter skelter, fell into a well in a corner of the ground resulting in more than a hundred of them dying that way. Estimates of those killed in Jalianwala Baug varied between 400 and 1500.

But, those deaths didn't go waste. The massacre at Jalianwala Baug fuelled a surge of widespread anger against the British, leading to the non-cooperation movement of 1920–22. Some historians consider that with Jalianwala Baug, the count-down for the end of British rule in India started. Jalianwala Baug was not only a watershed event in India's history, but also one which pricked the world conscience, and in 2019, Britain expressed "deep regret" for the incident.

We spent some time in the solemn environments of Jalianwala Baug. I felt, the place was still reverberating with the sound of the gun shots and the cries of the hapless victims echoing from there.

So many stories, folklores and historical facts connected with a river! No wonder, River Sindhu has a unique place among the rivers in this world.

Bidding good bye to the historic city of Amritsar, we reached Ladak. Here we could see the Indian part of River Sindhu as it flowed down the mountain ranges. This place is always enveloped in mist. To make amends for conducting the last rites of my father some fifty years ago using a small stream near my house as a 'proxy' for Sindhu, I wanted to get down here into the real Sindhu and re-do the rites; but, under the prevailing extreme cold conditions which prohibited entry into the river, I had to make do with an improvised version. I scooped up some water with both hands and raised it as if offering toast, and whispered: *"I beg for the forgiveness of the sins - if any - my beloved father might have committed, knowingly or unknowingly, during his time on this earth; and for the eternal salvation of his soul. For that, I dip in Sindhu, the holy river."* Then I poured it on my head.

# KAVERI
## Nursery of Tamil Culture

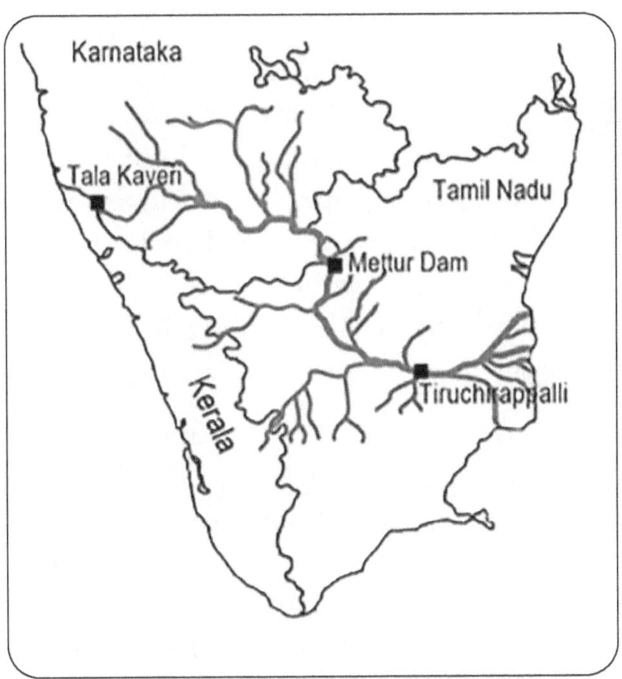



**Kaveri River**

River Kaveri is the most prominent among all the rivers of South India. For this populace dominated by the Dravidian race, Kaveri is revered on par with Ganga, the river which is considered holy by the entire country. As I started writing about Kaveri, being a South Indian myself, I can feel words from my pen beginning to gush down like the Kaveri in spate.

Kaveri originates at a place called Brahmagiri in Kodagu in Karnataka and ends up in the Bay of Bengal at a place called Poompuhar in Tamil Nadu. The total length of Kaveri is roughly 800 km, out of which 320 km is in Karnataka, 416 km is in Tamil Nadu and 64 km is in-between these two States. Thus, though Kaveri's birthplace is in Karnataka, she is flowing more through the nearby Tamil Nadu, and caters to the water needs of a large percentage of the people as well as farms in Tamil Nadu. No wonder, Kaveri is closer to the heart of the people of Tamil Nadu than any other State. Kaveri is omnipresent in most epics from folklores to folksongs to even the film songs of Tamil Nadu.

Perhaps it was due to Kaveri's presence in a multitude of film songs that, she came to occupy a place in my mind since childhood. As years rolled by, that bond got strengthened when I came to know about the annual music festival 'Thyagaraja Aaradhana' held on the banks of Kaveri at Tiruvaiyaru in Thanjavur District, Tamil Nadu. Later, a song about Kaveri "Sreeranga Nadhanin…" written by none other than Vali, the most loved and respected poet by the Tamil masses, in Ilayaraja's music in the Tamil film 'Mahanadi' made a permanent place for Kaveri in my heart.

My very first meeting with Kaveri was during my honeymoon five decades ago. I distinctly remember standing on a hillock near the starting point of the river at 'Thalaikkaveri'. My excitement at seeing the birthplace of the heroine of many a folk stories and songs was beyond description. My next meeting with Kaveri was years later when I went to Thiruvaiyar to participate in the 'Thyagaraja Aaradhana'. I have often felt that Kaveri has something special in her making her appear more alluring every time I met her.

The banks of Kaveri nurtured many ethnicities. They were also the venue of many a historical events from battles to festivals to cultural functions. Kaveri is the darling of the poets and artists too. They all sing her praise unreservedly. The heart-wrenching cries of Kannaki, the heroine of the epic Chilappathikaram following husband Kovilan's tragic end, are still lingering in the air along the banks of Kaveri.

For me, Kaveri is a young, beautiful, bubbly, village girl running around with milk for the grass on the river banks, and also for the saplings on the farms as described about Kerala's River Periyar by none other than the famous Kerala poet, the respected ONV.

Thinking about Kaveri, Mr S. K. Pottekkad, the renowned writer and traveller also comes to my mind. It was to the tranquil environs of Kaveri's birthplace at Brahmagiri in the Western Ghats; a place perpetually wrapped in lush greenery and the aroma of coffee flowers that Mr Pottekkad used to go to write his novels.

Born as a spring at Thalaikkaveri at Brahmagiri, River Kaveri's baby steps are through the coffee and tea plantations in the Coorg region. As she goes further traversing the beautiful hills, she reaches Dubare to create an island at Nisargadhama. Here, the people worship Kaveri, seeing her as a deity. Appropriately, the government has converted this place into a tourist spot for the people to lap up nature's visual treat. At Bahumandal, some ten kilometres down from Thalaikkaveri, Kaveri meets with the Sooyajyothi stream and the Kanihai river. This is considered the first Triveni confluence of Kaveri.

From there, Kaveri reaches the famous Krishnarajasagar dam. This dam was built in 1932 by Krishnaraja Wodayar, the 4th of the Wodayar Royal dynasty of Mysore as a solution for the droughts the kingdom faced during his time. The dam's Chief Engineer was none other than Sir M. Viswesaraiyya. Fittingly, the government conferred Bharatha Rathna, the ultimate civilian honour on 'Sir MV' as he is known among his legion of admirers. Sir MV's birthday is observed as 'Engineers Day'.

Krishnarajasagar dam is 40 metres tall and 2620 metres long, and it irrigates nearly 50000 hectares of land. With a surface area of 130 sq. km, this dam caters to the Shivasamudram hydroelectric project which is among the largest hydroelectric projects in Asia. The power generated from here caters to the needs of Mysore, Bangalore and the Kolar Gold Fields. The dam which is at 12 km away from Mysore, also boasts of the guardianship of the famous Brindavan Gardens attracting around two million visitors annually.

Continuing with its journey from here, Kaveri reaches Ramganthit. Here, there is a famous bird sanctuary where birds from Siberia reaches in certain season. Kaveri receive them as guest and entertain them for few days as guest of houner. This is also a tourist destination with facilities for stay and recreational activities like boating.

From Ramganthit, Kaveri moves on to the historic town of Srirangapatinam, the place which witnessed the invasions of Hyder Ali; and later, his son Tippu Sulthan who finally surrendered to the war strategies of the 1st Duke of Willington, Sir Arthur Wellesley in a war fought right on the banks of Kaveri.

Kaveri splits into two at Srirangapatinam, with both the branches flowing on either side of the Perumal Temple to create an island; but, only to re-join at Kaveri Sangamam. The authorities have put up a Nandi statue there. This place is renowned for performing 'Balitharpanam', the death rituals as per Hindu belief.

Continuing with its onward journey, what awaits Kaveri further down is a second Kaveri Sangamam where Kaveri is joined by the River Kabani coming from Kerala, and also the 'Spadika' river which is flowing subterranean. Still moving on, at the end of its 45 km journey from its origin, Kaveri reaches Thalakkad where, in the summer season, one can see eye-catching white sand dunes providing an enchanting sight to the visitors.

Moving on, Kaveri reaches Shivasamudram. There are two waterfalls there – Gaganachukki and Barachukki. This place is within a two hour drive from Bangalore. The waterfalls and fountains here provide unforgettable visual treats. As can only be expected, in this location, one can often see film units. Kaveri is not very deep here. Maybe because of that, people here use circular 'Kutta vanchis' or basket boats made of braided bamboo splinters and rubber sheets instead of the usual narrow, long wooden boats. Kutta vanchis are slow-moving; but are much safer, and with low draft, ideal for shallow waters.

Next on Kaveri's travel path is the Mekkethat dam, (Mekha Dhatu in Tamil) at Ram Nagar. Since her flow from here is through deep, narrow gorges between the hills, she moves here much faster. The river which was 150 metres wide at Trivenisangamam gets squeezed down to 10 metres at Mekkethat.

Hogganakkal waterfall is a famous waterfall at the border between the Dharmapuri district of Tamil Nadu and the Chamaraja Nagar district of Karnataka. This too is a very renowned tourist destination. One of the main attractions there, is the boating using ‹Kutta vanchis› mentioned early.

Bidding goodbye to Karnataka at Hogganakkal, Kaveri enters Tamil Nadu where many call her ‹Kaviri›. Maybe, Tamil people who are so proud of their language found this name conforming to pure Tamil dialect more than 'Kaveri.› There she flows further to Mettur in the Dharmapuri district to be received by the Mettur dam. This dam is 54 metres tall and 1600 metres long. The area of its reservoir is 42 sq. km. This was built in the 1930s under the supervision of an engineer by name Colonel W. M. Ellis. Fittingly, attached to the dam, there is a park named Ellis park.

Going further, Kaveri reaches Erode. By now, she has covered nearly half of her journey. At Erode, awaiting her is one more Trivenisangamam with Amudayar and River Bhavani joining Kaveri. It is here that the famous Sangameswar Temple is located. One of the main attractions here is the temple on the bank of Kaveri which people say, won›t get submerged however high the water in Kaveri may rise.

But, unfortunately, it is here that Kaveri gets polluted most. Most of the textile-based industrial units in Tamil Nadu are concentrated in and around Erode. This area has a near monopoly for factories engaged in weaving to the production of finished apparel for domestic as well as for export markets, thus providing jobs for thousands. The downside of it is that, the three hundred odd textile mills at Pallipalayam and Kumarapuram villages lying between Erode and Namakkal towns are constantly polluting Kaveri. Add to it, another 300 odd big bleaching units, some 170 dyeing units, and 37 tanneries near Erode to give you a fair picture of the extent of pollution Kaveri has to endure.

Tanneries, processing raw leather coming from the slaughterhouses extensively use chemicals containing harmful chromium etc, which, when discharged into the river pollutes not only the river water but, also the springs and wells over a wider area. The paradox here is that, it is from this very same river that the city water supply schemes draw water. Erode takes 34 million litres of water every day from Kaveri to meet its drinking water needs. Perhaps, as if in atonement for the sin of polluting the river, there are also nearly two hundred Siva Temples built in the villages along the banks of this river.

Next in her journey, at a place called Kodumudi, Kaveri which was flowing towards the southern direction till then, takes a turn towards east. Flowing further, River Amaravati joins Kaveri at Karoor. Then she passes through Kuzhithalai and heads towards Thiruchirappally. There is a dam here by name Mukkodu. This dam was built during the British rule. Its Engineer was Sir Arthur Cotton. Here again, Kaveri splits into two, and reaches Srirangam.

It is to Thanjavoor, to fulfil her life's mission of supplying the 'water of life' to the rice bowl of Tamil Nadu there, that Kaveri marches on from Srirangam. Here, her role as the caring deity who feeds her people manifests, and makes the whole world understand why the people of Tamil Nadu loves her so much. Thanjavur, Thiruchirappally and Srirangam, the cradles of South Indian culture depend heavily on Kaveri for their sustenance; and, but for Kaveri, they wouldn't have been what they are today. The Brihadeeswarar temple at Thanjavur, known as Thanjai Periya Kovil or Rajarajeswaram has a place among UNESCO's World Heritage Sites. This Shiva temple, arguably the biggest and tallest in India built in the tenth century by King Rajaraja Cholan of the Chola dynasty is a proud illustration of Dravidian architecture. This is also believed to be the only temple built entirely in granite.

There is yet another reason for Thanjavoor and Kaveri attracting world attention. Tiruvaiyaru, the venue of the world-famous annual Thyagaraja music festival is in the Thanjavur district. Maybe because of this, Kaveri appears to be moving rather slowly in this stretch. Can't blame her because, who will be in a hurry to leave the place echoing the religious music and song 'Jagadananda karaka' in 'Nattaraga', and 'Enthrey Mahanubhavalu', the fifth song in 'Sriragam'?

Kaveri flows into Kallanai at Thanjavoor. Built in the 1st century AD by a King of the Chola Dynasty, King Karikala Cholan, Kallanai is the first ever dam to be built in India. It was renewed by the British in the 19th century, and renamed the 'Grand Dam'. Still functional, this is one of the oldest irrigation projects in the world. This 19 centuries old dam survived as an engineering marvel till today, and stands with its heads high shaming the Kuttiyadi dam of the 20th century which started leaking within one year of its commissioning; not to mention the road over-bridge at Palarivattom of the 21st century which had to be rebuilt within two years of its inauguration. As a civil engineer specialising in dam design, I can't move on without paying rich tributes to King karikala Cholan.

Talking about King Karikala Cholan, in Srirangam also there are remnants of the great King's innovations still standing out as testimony to his greatness as a king. History says that the King constructed a protection wall along the low-lying areas on the banks of Kaveri from Srirangam to Poompuhar to protect his subjects and their crops and livestock from surging floodwaters. River Kollidam is a distributary of river Kaveri formed as it flows through the delta of Thanjavoor.

Finally, though reluctantly, from Thanjavoor, Kaveri moves on to fulfil her other duties further downstream. But, in that process, as if in distress over leaving her favourite Thanjavoor, she splits into five distributaries named Vetter, Arisalar, Koodamuruttiyar, Vennar, and with the fifth one flowing towards Kumbhakonam retaining the name Kaveri.

But, by the time she leaves Kumbhakonam, Kaveri looks a bit rejuvenated. She seems to have overcome her grief of leaving Thanjavoor, reconciling with the universal law 'all the nice things also will have an end', and flows towards east. Three rivers from Kerala; Kabini from Wayanad,

Bhavani from Palghat and Pambar from Idukki are joining Kaveri at different places during this phase of her travel.

At Nagapattinam, River Kollidam which had split with Kaveri at the delta of Thanjavoor, re-joins Kaveri after taking a detour through Chidambaram. From here, Kaveri heads towards Poompuhar.

## POOMPUHAR

Poompuhar occupies a prominent place in the historical as well as socio-cultural fields of Tamil Nadu. When the famous Rajendra Cholan was ruling Poompuhar, he built a port at a place Kaveri Poompattinam to facilitate the participation of his State in world trade. For centuries, Kaveri Poompattinam was the leading centre of trade in India. This place is also famous as an important place in Chilappathikaram. But, unfortunately, today, that port is only in the history books. It is believed that it was consumed by the sea in the fifth century AD following a massive natural calamity. The remnants of that old city are still lying submerged in the sea at a distance of 6 km from the shore. Many historians, history students and even inquisitive commoners visit this place.

Masilamaninathar Temple and the Chilappathikaram art gallery are the main attractions at Poompuhar. Masilamaninathar Temple built in the 14th century is an example of the excellence of the construction during those days. Chilappathikaram Art Gallery is a seven-story building having walls with sculptures representing scenes from Chilappathikaram. 'The place where the river joins the sea' is the meaning of the word Poom-har.

Kaveri is ending her journey here. What all could River Kaveri have witnessed during her existence since time immemorial? After taking birth as a small spring in Coorg, rivers Bhavani, Kabani, Amaravathi, Hemavathi, Pambar etc joined her on her way to reach Tiruvaiyyar. From there, she continued her travel, taking with her some smaller rivers and streams to become a massive river passionately called Akhanda Kaveri to finally merge with the sea at Poompuhar.

When we think about Kaveri, the name of the mythological character Pushkaran who loved rivers more than himself will also come to our mind. The only boon Pushkaran requested from lord Shiva after his arduous penance was to give him the power to live in the rivers and purify them. Maha Pushkaram is the festival in memory of Pushkaran. Legend has it that, like King Mahabali in the folk stories of Kerala, Pushkaran will come to visit each river once every year. The timing for that visit depends on the birth star of that river. For example, he visits the River Ganga in the Zodiac, River Narmada in Aries, River Saraswati in Gemini and River Kaveri in Libra, the birth stars of those rivers according to mythology. In each river, Pushkaram is celebrated once in every 12 years, and Mahapushkaram is celebrated once in every 144 years.

Many dismiss these as myths. Nevertheless, in the year 2017, from September 12th to 24th, believers celebrated the Kaveri Maha Pushkaram which was last held 144 years ago. That function was held at Mayiladumthura, on the banks of Kaveri. During those 12 days, Maha Pushkaram was celebrated at other places on the banks of Kaveri like Thalaikaveri, Srirangam, Thirupparai Grand dam, Tiruvaiyar, Kumbhakonam, and Poompuhar also.

Kaveri Maha Pushkaram celebrations involved filling a huge vessel with water; and after the customary prayers, sprinkling that holy water on the devotees. Side by side, they had put up a huge statue of mother Kaveri and a makeshift shamiana on the river bank. During the festivities on all of those 12 days, there were offerings, prayers, music, songs, dances etc as prescribed in the epics. The devotees also took dip in the river as part of the proceedings.

Today, River Kaveri has got some 60 medium and large irrigation projects, and nearly 2000 km of canals to take the water to the agricultural lands far away. Many of them were built a long time back. But, of late, sadly, the Kaveri River basin is shrinking in area. The principal reason for this is uncontrolled sand mining and encroachments. Inaction on the part of the government is facilitating this. People have begun organising protests against this. They fear that, at this rate, Kaveri may die a premature death.

Add to these, the pollution from the industries on its banks at Erode, Salem etc; and one can easily conclude that, the fears of the people are not unfounded.

Kaveri river dispute, involving Karnataka and Tamil Nadu as the main contenders; but, also with Pondicherry and Kerala on the fringes, is an ongoing one since 1892. Water is a divine gift from nature. Without it, life can't sustain. Each living being on this earth has an equal right to it. But, unfortunately, driven by greed, humans fight among themselves to establish supremacy over it. Many discussions followed by accords and agreements were reached on Kaveri, but they all were short-lived. Tribunal awards, court decisions etc ended up in widespread agitations. Later, the Kaveri Water Management Authority, and Kaveri Water Regulation Authority were set up to find a solution to the dispute. As per an understanding reached, out of an estimated 740 tmc of the Kaveri water, Karnataka will get 284.75 tmc, Tamil Nadu will get 433.75 tmc, Kerala will get 30 tmc, and Pondicherry will get 7 tmc. Another 10 tmc is reserved for environmental activities. Hopefully, this accord will stay.

An interesting development around River Kaveri is that, studies are on to connect her to River Godavari. In phase one of this plan, the surplus water from Godavari will be directed to Kaveri. The plan may sound fine; but, many technical issues are questioning its viability. The expert committee has submitted some proposals to the central government. Hopefully, something workable will emerge soon. Once this plan succeeds, that will be a shot in the arm for that grandiose plan to interlink rivers Brahmaputra, Ganga, Suvarnarekha and Mahanadi; and it will be the harbinger of many other projects like this. That way, let all the rivers get interconnected for the benefit of all. Once that happens, there won't be any water scarcity in any part of the country, thus paving the way for more agriculture production, more employment; and above all, bringing permanent peace and harmony on the banks of our rivers.

Let us thank God for giving us River Kaveri, and pray for her to continue to flow majestically till eternity, serving our future generations also remembering the words of wisdom "we didn't inherit the earth from our forefathers, but, borrowed it from the future generations."

# KRISHNA

## Lifeblood of the Rice-bowl of South India

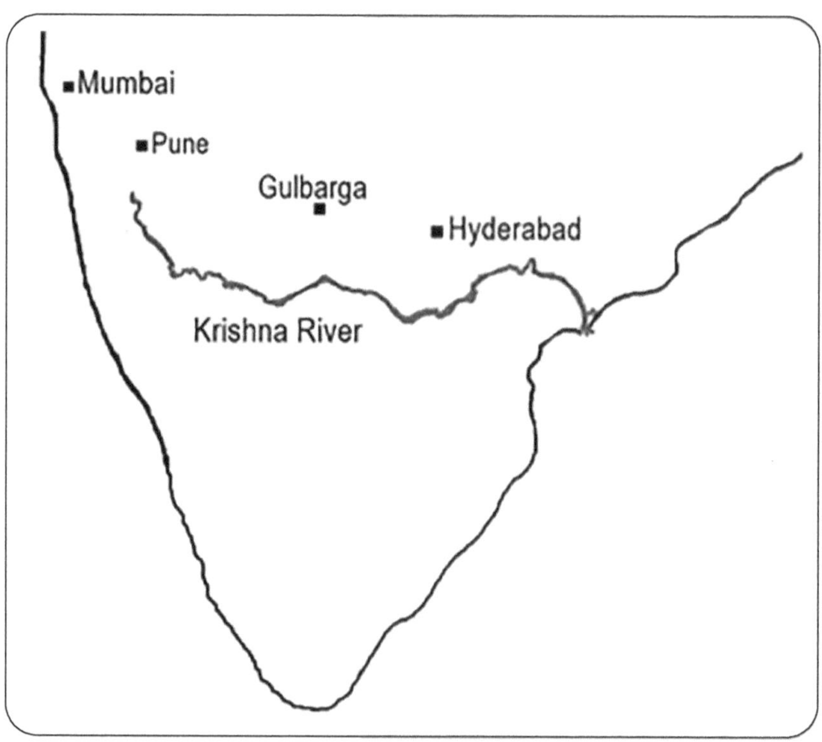



**Krishna River**

River Krishna is originating at a place just 64 km away from the Arabian Sea on the west coast; and like her all Indian sisters, she too was destined to join a sea. So, one would have expected her to reach the Arabian Sea overnight. But, that was not to be. Her calling was to travel some 1300 km traversing through 4 Indian States to reach another sea, the Bay of Bengal on the east coast of India.

River Krishna's birthplace is in the Jor village in the Western Ghat ranges in Western Maharashtra, at an altitude of 1337 metres. Flowing down, she first turns south, then goes east to get into Karnataka, and then to Andhra Pradesh and Telangana before merging with the Bay of Bengal. She took this arduous route across India to fulfil her life's mission of quenching the thirst of not only millions of parched throats; but also thousands of hectares of farmlands. Krishna river basin extends to over an area of 2,59,000 sq. km. That is almost 8% of the river basins in India. Quite deservedly, she is also called 'Half-Ganga'. The peculiarity of the Krishna River basin is the bio-diversity of its soil. Place to place, it varies from acidic to alkaline. You can also see red earth and sandy soil; and even aggregates of laterite in the region.

After River Godavari, River Krishna is the second longest river in South India. On an all-India basis, there is only one river, Ganga, longer than these two. Krishna's tributaries Koyna, Warna, Panchaganga, Dhudgana, Ghadaprabha, Malaprabha, Tungabhadra etc join her from one side, whereas; Yarla, Musi, Maneru, Bhima etc join her from the other. Size-wise, Tungabhadra is the largest among the tributaries, whereas; lengthwise, that credit goes to Bhima. Tributaries Panchaganga, Warna and Yarla join Krishna at Sangli in Maharashtra. This is considered a holy place. It was near this place that sage Dattatreya sat on penance. Almaty dam is here. Near this, the River Malaprabha joins Krishna. After that, Tungabhadra, and then Bhavanasi joins Krishna.

Krishna water irrigates some 200000 sq. kilometres which is more than 10% of India's land area under agriculture. Though the estimated annual flow in River Krishna was an impressive 78 cubic kilometres, that was insufficient to meet the growing water needs of the region. So, in 2016, River Krishna was connected to River Godavari through a canal at a place Polavaram. This is known as the Pattiseema lift irrigation scheme. With this, water became available in the Prakasam Bara district of Andhra

Pradesh, and the region became one of the biggest rice-producing areas of India. This is also known as the Prakasam Barrage area.

The bond between the rivers and India's spiritual heritage is inseparable. The places selected by the great sages to put up their hermitages, and to impart knowledge to the upcoming generation were invariably on the banks of the rivers. So also, most of the temples. River Krishna too can boast of many such institutions. Sreesailam of Dwadasha heritage and the Buddist centre of learning Nagarjunakonda are among them. The Maha Ganapathi Mandiram and the Kasi Viswesara temple are some of the prominent pilgrim centres on the banks of River Krishna. However, the holy place of yesteryears Sangameswaram is now lying submerged in the Shreesailam reservoir for most of the year. Only when the water level there goes down, devotees can gain access to that place as briefed to me by my friend Mr. Krishna Reddy Pollution Control Board engineer,

On the banks of Krishna, one can see many more holy places. The Veerabhadra temple at Lepakshi, the Kanaka Durga Temple at Vijayawada, and the Mallikarjuna temple at Srisailam are some of them. The biggest attraction in River Krishna is the huge granite temple across the river at Bhillawadi in Maharashtra built some 240 years ago. Apart from these, there are the Dattamandir Ksheera Lingeswara temple and the Venkateswara temple near the confluence of River Bhima with River Krishna. There are some temples at the Agrahara Ghat also. Among the other attractions are, the Gana Saraswati temple and Patala Ganga ghat along the river bank.

Further, like what we saw in 2017 with River Kaveri, along the banks of River Krishna also they had celebrated the Pushkara festival in the year 2016, from August 12 to 23 to match the birth star of River Krishna. Functions were held at Vijayawada Ghat, Padmavati Ghat, Krishnaveni Ghat, Durga Ghat, Patala Ganga Ghat, Chiklode Ghat, Raichur Ghat etc.

There are many waterfalls in River Krishna. Ethi Pothala, Ghod Chinna Malakke, Gokh Malla Theertham etc are prominent among them. There are some huge bridges also across this river. The Krishna bridge at Vay in Maharashtra, Irvin bridge at Sangli, Amgali bridge, also near Sangli,

Kudachi bridge, Bisowndati bridge at Sounda rai baug, Tangadagi bridge, Jabagi bridge etc figure among them.

River Krishna is rich in the case of dams also. Dham dam, Hippargi barrage, Almatti dam, Narainpur dam, Bhima dam, Jurala dam, Srisailam dam, Nagarjuna sagar dam, Pulichintala dam, Prakasam barrage, Tungabhadra dam, Rajoli Bandra barrage, Sangekkula barrage etc are the most prominent among them. Mulsha dam, Thokkarwadi dam, Ujjain dam Bhadra dam, Jurala Hydro-electric project, Lower Jurala Hydro-electric project etc are also projects in River Krishna. Altogether, there are more than a dozen hydroelectric projects in this river. The projects at Srisailam and Koyna are massive with production capacities of 1670 MW and 1920 MW respectively. It must be mentioned that in the case of the Almaty dam, there are some disputes between Andhra Pradesh and Karnataka.

River Krishna supplies water to the cities and towns like Vijayawada, Guntur, Flouro Machilipatanam, Kakinada, some towns in the East Godavari district etc. What is most commendable is that, though the River Krishna is flowing only through four States, the Krishna water reaches a fifth State, Tamil Nadu. It is on River Krishna that Chennai city, the capital of Tamil Nadu depends on drinking water. This project is known as the 'Telugu Ganga Project'.

The banks of the main tributary of River Krishna, Tungabhadra are rich in history. Vijayanagaram, South India's biggest empire in the middle ages was on the banks of Tungabhadra. Its remnants are still visible at Humpy, the biggest city in those days. Tungabhadra has an alias 'Pamba' giving credence to the argument that the river mentioned as 'Pamba' in the Ramayana story is Tungabhadra; not the River Pamba of Kerala as believed by some in Kerala.

It is on the bank of River Musi, another tributary of Krishna that the twin city of Hyderabad – Secendarabad is built. The famous Charminar, built in the year 1591 by Khuli Khubsha is also on the bank of the River Musi. It is said that Charminar was built in jubilation, and also as an offering to God for the eradication of the Plague. Charminar has, as the name indicates four minars – towers – supposed to be representing the four Khalifas of the Islamic religion.

The cities and towns on the banks of Krishna deserve particular mention. The biggest city on the banks of Krishna is Vijayawada, previously known as Baswada. Legend has it that Arjun, one of the heroes of the epic Mahabharatha observed penance on Indrakeeladri hills, following which Lord Indra gave him the Pasupathastram which played the cardinal role in winning the Kurukshetra war for the Pandavas. The meaning of the name Vijayawada is 'the place which earns you victory'. Myths apart, when the Chola king Rajaraja Cholan conquered Vijayawada, the city was named Rajendracholapuram. But, during the British rule, they changed it to Baswada. However, after India's independence, the city was rechristened Vijayawada. Prakasam barrage and the Kanakadurga temple are the main attractions in Vijayawada.

The Prakasam barrage is a standing testimony of the expertise of British military engineers. These days, we have many branches in engineering like civil, mechanical, electrical, computer, electronics, chemical, I.T, instrumentation etc. But, in those days, there were only two disciplines – civil (for civilian) engineering and military engineering. During the peace times, military engineers were deputed for civil engineering jobs. Many of our dams built during the pre-independence days were constructed by British military engineers; Captain Buckley, Captain Lakey, Captain Best etc, to name a few. The Prakasam Barrage is one such creation. It was one Major Kwantum, who proposed to the Director Board of the East India Company to construct this barrage. The Board approved it, and the barrage became a reality for two crores of rupees. It was in the year 1852 that the construction of this 1223-metre-long barrage started, and it was completed in three years. Many years later, in 1953, a bridge was built over the barrage, and the barrage and the bridge got named after Mr. T. Prakasam, the first Chief Minister of Andhra Pradesh. This barrage irrigates 1.2 million acres of land.

There are many national parks also along the banks of River Krishna. Chandoli, Kuthirmukh, Kasubrahmananda Reddy National Park,

Mahavir Harina Vasanthali National Park, Mrugavani National Park etc are prominent among them. The Khattaprabha Bird Sanctuary, Gudavi Bird Sanctuary, Great India Bird Sanctuary etc also are there on the banks of Krishna.

In modern times, rivers have become bones of contention not only between countries; but even between States within a country. River Krishna is not different. On April 10, 1969, the Central Government appointed a Commission to resolve the difference between the States on the rivers Krishna and Godavari. This was as per the Interstate River Water Dispute Act 1956 (IRWD Act). On May 27, 1976, the Commission submitted the report on River Krishna which runs in Maharashtra, Karnataka, and the undivided Andhra Pradesh. Krishna river basin is 259000 sq. km, out of which 68000 sq. km is in Maharashtra, 116000 sq. km in Karnataka and 75000 sq. km in Andhra Pradesh. As per the Commission's recommendation, each one of these States was to get a certain percentage of Krishna water. This Tribunal had also stipulated that a review of this agreement can be made only in 2050. However, with the splitting of Andhra Pradesh into Andhra Pradesh and Telangana in 2014, new disputes have come to the fore. They remain unresolved till date.

Universally, rivers take the brunt of the harmful effects of industrialisation. Krishna's fate is not different. Effluents from the factories of big cities like Pune, Satara, Kolhapur, Hyderabad, Kurnool, Vijayawada etc pollute River Krishna and her tributaries extensively. It is into Moola-Mootha, a tributary of Krishna that the discharges from Pune municipality flow. River Musi, another tributary takes the waste from Hyderabad - Secendarabad combine. I was involved in the effluent treatment efforts of the Pattancheru area some thirty years back. The Gwalior Rayons factory on the banks of Tungabhadra is discharging most of its effluents into the river leaving the river water blackish and smelly; the same way the sister unit of that factory at Kozhikode was doing to Chaliyar river in Kerala for 40 years till its closure in 1999 rendering the water there unfit for drinking, washing or even farming. To give an idea of the extent of that pollution, the Biochemical Oxygen Demand (BOD), the yardstick for water pollution was 300 mg/l in the river against the permitted 30mg/l, and the BOD of the discharges from the factory was 1000 mg/l.

These days, in many towns along River Krishna, there are associations of nature lovers to keep a watch over pollution, encroachments and all kinds of abuses of the river. Together with the Andhra Pradesh Pollution Control Board, these associations have been able to curb the abuse of River Krishna to some extent. Even then, the data coming out of river water analysis is showing an alarming increase in pollution. Of late, it is noticed that the proportion of chemical wastes is on the increase, and there is more untreated wastewater coming into the river. Recently, Andhra Pradesh Pollution Control Board found that the water in many of the State's rivers was unfit for consumption.

Evidently, our river management schemes – not only in pollution control; but, also in the overall management of this invaluable resource - are not at all efficient. Our rivers cause flooding on their banks during the rainy season, but, go dry without even drinking water during the summer months. If the dreams of interlinking rivers materialise, this problem could be addressed to a great extent. The central government has set up a task force for this. They have already initiated steps for reaching an understanding with various States on how to go about with the implementation of the river linking schemes.

Godavari – Kaveri interlinking is planned in two stages. In the first stage, the surplus water of the River Godavari is to be directed to the River Kaveri without harming the interests of various stakeholders. The task force has prepared a Detailed Project Report (DPR) for this. Still, it will require a lot more studies on the technical, financial and practical sides of it all, before one can say the project is 'on'. The second stage of the project is the 'mother of all river linking projects'; which is linking Brahmaputra – Ganga – Suvarnarekha – Mahanadi – Godavari.

Let us hope, one day, all these projects would become a reality. Once that happen, we will have the holy water of Ganga from the Himalayas up above flowing in the Nilas and Pambas down south. Not only that; with this, the quarrel between the States on sharing of water would also become a thing of the past.

Krishna is another name for Droupathi, the heroine of the epic Mahabharatha who had to wander through the forests for twelve years enduring the pain of public humiliation. The same lady, who, with her burning desire to take revenge upon the Kauravas for the insult, empowered and energised the Pandavas into destroying the Kauravas. I have often felt that our rivers, the victims of the greed and power struggles of men are very much like Droupathi. One can only hope that these rivers won't turn against us with the same fury with which Droupathi turned against Kauravas.

# BRAHAMPUTRA

# The Only 'Manly' River

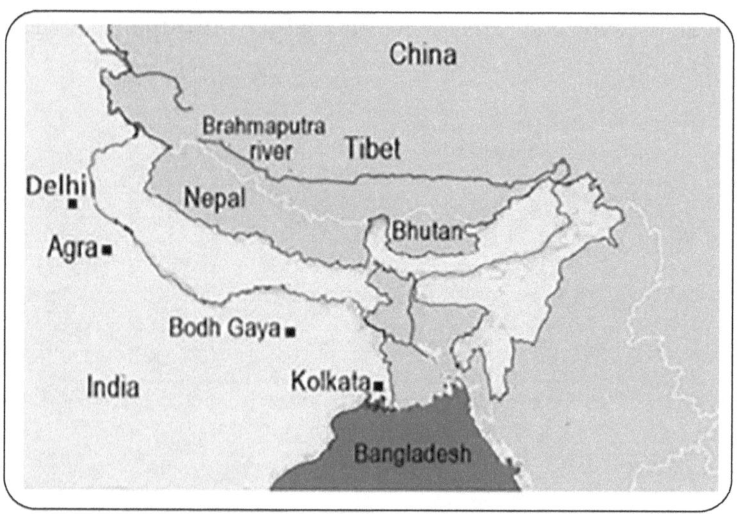

**Brahmaputra River**

## Scene 1

The venue – The porch of a hotel in Frankfurt, Germany. Time, 11 pm. A taxi pulls in, and a slim, 70 years old, weary-looking man, along with his baggage gets dropped there. After loading his baggage into a trolley, he looks around; but there is no human being to be seen anywhere to guide him. He pulls and pushes the handle of the door to the lobby, but it refuses to budge. Standing there feeling forlorn, his eyes fall on the instructions on a computer screen put up near the door. As advised in it, he searches for the booking confirmation in his phone and finds out a password. After a few seconds' hesitations, he nervously types that password into the computer keyboard; and to his great relief, the door to the dimly lit hotel lobby opens. He staggers into the lobby. Enveloped in the eerie silence reminiscent of a burial ground at midnight, the atmosphere there was frightening.

No reception counter; not even a soul to be seen in the lobby either. He looks around and finds on a tripod at the centre of the lobby, a board with directions for the guests displayed prominently. Spending a few minutes studying what to do next, he gets into the lift and reaches his room floor. There he locates his room, and types the password on the keypad on the door very carefully, fearing the consequences; should his shivering finger foul up things. Thank God, the door to the room opens for him. He darts in throws his baggage aside and dives into the bed. Within no time he slips into a deep slumber.

## Scene 2

The venue - a stretch of tea gardens in Assam, India. Time, afternoon. A brand new Mahindra Scorpio Jeep hurtles through the half-paved estate roads. There, in its back seat sits a slim 70 years old man sandwiched between two machine gun-wielding tough-looking guys.

Surprised? That was not the screenplay of a thriller movie. It was me who was the slim old man in both the above scenes. I was on travel for an official visit as the Assessor to perform a sustainability and environmental system Principal Auditor in a the famous Assam Frontier Tea Garden on behalf of the reputed company American Bureau of Industrial Verification. That first scene was from the first part of that long journey which started in Stockholm, the capital of Sweden and ended in a hotel in Frankfurt for a transit halt. My confusion at the hotel in Frankfurt was due to my unfamiliarity with the ultra-modern fully automatic 'check-in' procedures of that 'self-service' hotel. However, it all ended well for me.

But, if you thought that the second scene was that of me being kidnapped by some terrorists, you are wrong. There, I was being treated to the 'black cat' VIP security which my hosts, the Frontier Tea Garden Assam had arranged for me at the airport at Assam when I reached there for the last leg of my travel by road to the tea estate. That tea estate was close to the India-Myanmar border which was a stronghold of the Assam Insurgents. Since I was representing an American company, my value as a hostage will be huge. That was the reason why my hosts didn't want to take any chances with my security.

You may now wonder why I took up this risky assignment at all. The fact was, I volunteered to accept this assignment after many of my colleagues in TUV-Nord and American audit group backed off fearing the dangers involved. Another deterrent to them was, this audit stretching nearly three weeks covering eight estates was an arduous one. But, for me, both these negatives were inducements because, going to that risky area giving me the aura of a hero apart, in those three weeks, I will have plenty of spare time for spending with River Brahmaputra; that too, when the audit dates were to coincide with the Mahapushkara festival of Brahmaputra.

For me, seeing the Brahmaputra River was one of my long-cherished ambitions. However, it was remaining unfulfilled because going all the way to Assam only to see a river was a bit foolhardy. But, now, linked with an official visit, I found it as a heaven-sent opportunity, and grabbed it with both hands. Although, for that, I had to travel a distance thrice the 3969 km which the Brahmaputra travels though in Tibet, China, India and Bangla Desh.

My journey was long and arduous. It was at around 7 pm that I started off on this trip from Stockholm, the city which, in 1972 hosted the first World Conference on Environment. From there, by around 9.30 pm, I reached Frankfurt. My next flight was to Abu Dhabi, but that was only at 6 am the next day. That was why I stayed there in that Frankfurt hotel for the night. Abu Dhabi was 5000 km away. From there, my final destination Dibrugarh is another 4850 km, touching Bombay and Calcutta on the way. With connection flights within a couple of hours, I didn't have to take a stop-over anywhere else.

As I came out of the arrival hall at the Dibrugarh airport, a representative of the Assam Frontier Tea Gardens was waiting there with a placard with my name on it in one hand, and a bouquet in the other. Reaching the jeep, I was surprised at seeing the security guards who, ignoring my preference for the window seat, politely directed me to occupy the rear middle seat, with them on either side protecting me.

TheAssam Frontier Tea Gardens Company is there since the pre-independence days. Most of the tea estates here are owned by them. I was accommodated in one of the bungalows reserved for managers. Universally, the managers' bungalows in the tea estates are the ultimate word in living comfort and luxuries. Swimming pool, tennis court, squash court; what not? Not only all the material luxuries; but also servants, cooks, gardeners, drivers, you say anything, people for all kinds of services. But, as an exception, in my case there was an irritant; the presence of those overzealous security guards.

However, with nobody around for open communication, I found the stay in the bungalow too boring. The Tea Company was very receptive to my problem, and they soon shifted me to the bungalow of a Senior Manager Mr. Santosh Hazarika who happened to be a relative of Mr. Bhupan Hazarika, one of the most famous musicians in the history of Indian Cinema. I had a great time sharing the accommodation with him. Not only on music, I got a lot of information on the River Brahmaputra also from Mr. Hazarika.

River Brahmaputra, originating from the Himalayas, is a transboundary river which flows through Tibet, China, India, and Bangladesh. Brahmaputra is known as the Yarlung Tsangpo in Tibet, the Siang in Arunachal Pradesh, and Jamuna In Bangladesh. The Brahmaputra is also known by its Chinese name, Yarlung Zangbo. As this river reaches Arunachal Pradesh, it takes the name Siyang. As it moves further and takes in River Dipp and River Lohit, the river gets christened the Brahmaputra. For the Assamese, this river is Brahmadeven's son, the son who quarrelled with his father, transformed into a river and came down to the earth. So, unlike the other Indian rivers, the River Brahmaputra is masculine. It has a length of 3969 km, up to 10km in width, and a maximum depth of 128 metres. In Guwahati, it narrows down to less than 1 km. There are many bathing ghats in the Brahmaputra. Many people visit these ghats to perform various religious rituals.

Some of the bridges in the Brahmaputra are very famous. The Dhola Sadhiya bridge is one among them. Named after Mr. Bhuvan Hazarika, its length is 9.5 km; 3.5km longer than the Bandra sea link at Bombay. It is constructed in the Lohit River where it joins the Brahmaputra in Assam. This is the longest bridge in India. Among the other massive bridges in this river, is the Koyla Bhomura bridge built in 1987 at 3015 m long. The Saraighat bridge built in 1962 is 1492m.

The Brahmaputra is the backbone of farming activities in Assam. Needless to say, it also is the main source of fish for the Assamese. Many social customs of the Assamese are linked to the Brahmaputra Rriver. For example, preceding a marriage, the bride and her family will come to the river and collect some water in small pitchers. It is this water which will be used in the marriage rituals.

The Brahmaputra is also notorious for bringing misery to people. Unlike most other Indian rivers, due to the melting of snow in the Himalayas, this river experiences flooding even in the summer months causing widespread losses along its banks. The Brahmaputra is notorious for its undercurrents too. Once, a boat capsized in this river resulting in the death of nearly 40 people.

The Brahmaputra and its banks are rich in flora and fauna. There are numerous small and big islands in the Brahmaputra River providing ideal settings for biodiversity. Some of them are the habitats of golden monkeys. This region receives rainfall almost throughout the year. The principal crops there are maize, wheat, tea, pulses, oil seeds etc.

One interesting thing about the Brahmaputra is that, in this river, fishing is not the exclusive preserve of men. One can see many women also engaged in this; though using a different technique. Men usually use a spear-like tool to catch fish; whereas women's principal tool is a braided cane basket. The fishing boats in Assam are very broad towards the mid-section; different from the ones we see in most other States. One can also see multi-decked tour boats in the river.

It may be a bit unnerving to many of us to know that many areas of River Brahmaputra are also infested by crocodiles. Large size crocs of Marsh and Mugger varieties which grow to more than 18 feet were in this river at one time. However, due to pollution and human interference, many of them are facing extinction. Like in River Ganga, there are sweet water dolphins in River Brahmaputra also. Dolphins were plenty in this river at one time. Dolphin meat is in big demand in this region. But, due to poaching, and also due to the interference of the dams in their natural habitat and ecosystem, their numbers too are dwindling rapidly. It is said that at one time there were some two hundred varieties of aquatic life including turtles, brown trout, silver carp, and even sweet water sharks and salmons also in this river.

According to a study by the Botanical India Survey, Brahmaputhra's river mouths are also rich with some 4000 sq. kms occupied by mangroves and adjoining areas abound with biodiversity. Many endangered species of plant and animal life can be spotted there. Not to mention, the one-honed Rhinos, elephants, deer, leopards etc. Most of them are seen at the Namchaparva, Sangloong, Niyogi, Kangto, and Kavsang mountain ranges.

Coming to the cities on the bank of River Brahmaputra, at the top of the list is, of course, Guwahati, the capital of Assam, and the biggest town there. Guwahati is a 'must see' city in the itinerary of any traveller. It is in this region where the one-horned rhinos are concentrated. This place is also a leading commercial and educational centre of the North–East. In Guwahati, there are also historically important places like the Devi Kamakhya temple known for shaman practices and Buddhism.

Dibrugarh is another important city located in the middle of the tea gardens in Assam. Dibrugarh is rich in oil reserves, coal, natural gas and clay. One of the earliest oil exploration projects in India dating back to British days was near Dibrugarh where the head office of the modern day Oil India Ltd is located. Dibrugarh is also the most important educational centre in Assam.

Jorhat, which, in the 18th century was the capital of a country by the name Ahom, is another important town in Assam. People with diverse cultures are the inhabitants of this place which is an important commercial centre of Assam. The main attractions there now are its churches, gardens; even the cemeteries. The historically important Hindu temple Dhekiakhowa Bornamghar is also here. The Jorhat Theatre established in 1896 is the main venue of cultural events in this town. Mr. Birendrakumar Bhttacharya who is the very first Gnanapeedam awardee of Assam is from Jorhat. It is also in Jorhat that revolutionaries of the first freedom movement, Mr. ManiRam Diwan and Mr. Piyali Baruah were hanged publically. With the commissioning of the Jorhat Provincial Railway in 1885, the tea industry at Jorhat got a boost. Rain Forest Institute and Toklay Tea Research Institute are two of the nearly eight research institutes and universities here.

Tezpur, previously known as Sonitpur is another cultural centre of Assam. This town is on the Northern bank of Brahmaputra. During the winter months, the snow-covered mountain peaks here will appear more enchanting than even the Himalayan peaks. Tezpur has a nickname as the city of blood. There is a story behind this in the epics. Anirudhan, the grandson of Srikrishna fell in love with Usha, the daughter of Banasura, son of Mahabali. On knowing about this, an incensed Banasura hid Usha in a hill encircled by fire and imprisoned Anirudhan. In retaliation, Srikrishna declared war on Banasuran, and the fierce battle went on for days. It was in Tezpur that the battle was fought. There was so much bloodshed, the entire place got soaked in blood; and hence the name, the city of blood. Further, in this same story, that hill encircled by fire and aptly named Agnigud is a tourist attraction of Tezpur. Other attractions are the Mahabhairav temple, the Chitralekha garden built by the British Deputy Commissioner Mr. Cole, Trimurthi Garden, Rudrapada Temple, Bamuni Hills etc.

River Brahmaputra is relatively less polluted. However, recently there were reports of fish dying en-mas at some place, and arsenic pollution was suspected to be the cause. I had mentioned about arsenic pollution in the chapter 'Kaveri' in the context of pollution in River Kaveri due to the effluents from the industries at Erode. But, here in Brahmaputra, with industrial pollution ruled out, where from the arsenic could have come in? One likely reason for this is the arsenic from the rocks along the river bank getting mixed with the water, though it sounds too far-fetched. Mercifully, that was a one-off case; and hope, won't be repeated.

River linking being the in-thing these days, efforts are on for linking Brahmaputra with River Suvarnarekha and River Mahanadi. Once that materialises, it will benefit the upper regions of Assam, as well as the States of Bengal, Bihar, Jharkhand and Orissa. One thing we have to keep in mind while discussing the River Brahmaputra is that, this is an international river with China, Bangladesh and Bhutan having a finger in the pie with associated problems.

Incidentally, Bhutan is a country which has always been on friendly terms with India. There are scheduled bus services from the Esplanade station and the Dalhousie station of Culcatta to Thing Fu, the capital of Bhutan. These buses are run by the Bhutan tourism department. These buses leave Calcutta by dusk, and reach Thing Fu by the afternoon, the next day. The one-week tourist 'visa on arrival' will be stamped at the check-post at the border. During my Calcutta days for my post-graduation course, I had visited Bhutan using this channel.

Many of the tributaries of Brahmaputra are originating from the glaciers near the Kaila's Mountains. From there, they flow towards the east, and reach Arunachal Pradesh after many twists and turns, and traversing through deep mountain gorges. Tributaries Debang, Siyang and Lohit join Brahmaputra at Assam. Most of the tributaries of Brahmaputra are flowing through Bhutan which uses them extensively for the production of electricity. After Bhutan became independent in 1949, India has contributed a lot to its development. As per agreement signed between the two countries in 1961, a 27mw project was started in Jaldhakka, one of the tributaries of Brahmaputra. India has been very considerate towards Bhutan, and the various agreements between the two countries were always on very liberal terms for Bhutan. Also, it is mostly the Indian companies which executed those projects. The surplus electricity from these projects is also being bought by India.

Bangladesh got liberated from Pakistan in 1971 with India's help. However, though the general terms between India and Bangladesh are by and large cordial, when it comes to sharing the river waters, some friction is often visible. Bangladesh is a country which faces extreme drought during the summer season, and floods during the monsoon. The topography of the country together with poor planning are the reasons for it.

Brahmaputra is in spate as I am writing these lines. 62 people are reported to have died in floods in Assam this week. 700 villages were submerged by flood waters with some four lakh people becoming victims of the havoc caused by floods. More than 135000 people have reportedly taken shelter in the nearly 700 relief camps opened in the aftermath of the floods.

Shortage of appropriate travel facilities is the biggest challenge faced by the people in the North-East. Large-scale evacuation of people in the face of any natural calamities continues to be a near-impossible task. The central government is taking some steps to address this. The Bogilwil railroad bridge, the longest of its kind in India opened by Prime Minister Mr. Narendra Modi in December 2020 is one among them. Plans are afoot to build five more big bridges in the Brahmaputra for the same purpose.

That is not all. Cochin shipyard has recently received an order to build two dozen boats to be used as ferries in the Brahmaputra. These boats should put an end to the often heard boat capsize tragedies from there. My second niece, brillient naval architect Anjana, General Manager of Cochin Ship yard is engaged in the design of such special gigantic boats. Similarly, Spicejet, the airline company in India is heard to be at the drawing board to make seaplanes for use in the Brahmaputra. This will attract a lot of adventure tourists to the region, it is forecasted. Seaplanes are aeroplanes modified to take off and land in the water. They were originally developed for military purposes, but these days they are finding takers in the tourism industry also.

Over the past few years, it is observed that, at times, the Brahmaputra water reaching Arunachal Pradesh was found to have a blackish hue. It is suspected that this is caused by the activities connected with the drilling of tunnels in the upstream areas by the Chinese. The Arunachal govt. has brought this matter to the attention of the central govt.

The Brahmaputra River basin spread over China, India, Bangladesh and Bhutan is 580000 sq. km in area. Around 50% of it is in China, 34% in India, and 8% each in Bhutan and Bangladesh. To date, no water-sharing treaties exist between these stakeholders. The Chinese already have a huge dam somewhere at the start of the river. India is building one now on the Arunachal Pradesh – Assam border. It is reported that China is going to build another huge dam in the Midong district in Tibet as part of their 14th five-year plan for 2021-'25, and has earmarked 1.5 billion USD for it. It is also said that this project will go a long way for China in achieving 'carbon neutrality' by the year 2060. However, India has its apprehensions about the impact of this dam on India.

According to the World Bank, by the year 2023, India could surpass China in population. So, India will need more water, food, electricity etc. But, at the same time, China too will need more of the Brahmaputra water because most of their subterranean water, as well as river water, is contaminated. Water shortage is already felt in India and Bangladesh after the commissioning of the Sangmoo and Sangpo dams by China. That is going to aggravate with the construction of the proposed one. How these irritants are going to play out is a matter of conjectures. As per the latest statistics, the annual per-capita availability of potable water in 2021 is only one-fourth of what it was in 1947.

In the year 2000, following a dam collapse triggered by an earthquake in River Saying, a tributary of Brahmaputra, there was massive flooding and loss of lives and property in India. Following this, in the year 2002, an expert committee was constituted. The river water dispute between India and China had started way back in 1950. In 2017, there was a flare-up, and the Indian and Chinese forces took positions facing each other at the border of Bhutan. That led to some rifts in the Brahmaputra accord also. Escalations of tensions between the two countries had other ripple effects as well. China stopped sharing with India, the information on river water data. However, by 2018, it eased considerably, and normalcy was restored.

The benefits of linking Brahmaputra with the other rivers are huge. Controlling the floods apart, that will help better management of farming activities. So also, the improvements in the water transport systems. But, they have their downsides also. Its impact on the environment could be huge. It could submerge some places forever. The habitats of many species of animal, birds and plant life could disappear. Re-drafting of river water treaties between India, Nepal and Bangladesh also will become necessary.

India and Bangladesh share the water of nearly 50 big and small rivers. A comprehensive plan to link all of them will be highly beneficial to both the countries; no doubt. It was a British Engineer, Sir Arthur Cotton who floated first, the idea of linking the Indian rivers. He introduced it at the government level in 1870. In Kerala, it was Sir C.P. Ramaswamy Iyer who broached these ideas in 1926. That apart, in 1972, Engineer K.L. Rao, the Union Minister for Agriculture, submitted a detailed report on this. Indian river linking project plan envisages, 29 canals adding up to 9600 km.

Coming back to my visit to this region, as planned at the very start of this trip, during the breaks in my official duties I used to visit the banks of Brahmaputra, and collect as much information as possible by interacting with the locals and people in the know of things. It was during my stay in the estate that the Mahapushkara festival of Brahmaputra was held. So, I had the opportunity to participate in that also. The Mahapushkara festival of Brahmaputra is different from that of the other rivers. The festival now on, is happening after 144 years. I had a great time there. The banks of the river were brimming with festival spirit; reverberating with the chants and recitals of scriptures. The reflections of the tall mountain ranges rising majestically into the sky in the waters of Brahmaputra were a sight I will never forget. This visit to the Brahmaputra made me prouder about our cultural heritage.

But, this phase in my life was too good to last forever. My days on the estate had to be cut short by an unexpected development. One night, there was the theft of 40 large boxes of tea from the factory's store. Investigations revealed that the leader of one of the trade unions was behind it. So, the company management placed him under suspension. In, protest the workers went on strike and laid siege on the estate. Within just two days, the situation became explosive. The factory manager visited me and explained the situation. According to him, my inspection plans for the tea estates won't work out. I conveyed the information to Mr. Raghu Iyyangar, the General Manager of the certification company in Bombay. His instruction to me was to wind up and return as early as possible. Accordingly, arrangements were made for me to return the next day itself, and I left taking along with me the sweet memories of the River Brahmaputra.

From time immemorial, India was looked at with awe by the other countries. The reason was our unique cultural heritage, literature, social order, scriptures, philosophy and so on. Nowhere else in the world you can see people worshipping rivers, or treating rivers as Gods. That was rather symbolic; aimed at instilling in the masses, the importance of rivers in our existence. Unfortunately, consumed by selfish motives, the present generation seems to have no qualms about abusing the rivers to inflict irreversible damages on them even for petty personal gains. Due to reckless human interference, nature has lost its rhythm and balance reminding me of Gandhi's words "Earth provides enough to satisfy every man's needs; but, not every man's greed". No wonder, we are now up against el Nino, unpredictability of weather etc. Scientists say, the sea is rising due to global warming, and by the year 2050, many parts of India including Cochin and Mumbai could get submerged in the sea. Nature is striking back. Time is running out for corrective measures.

# GANGA

# For Salvation From All Your Sins

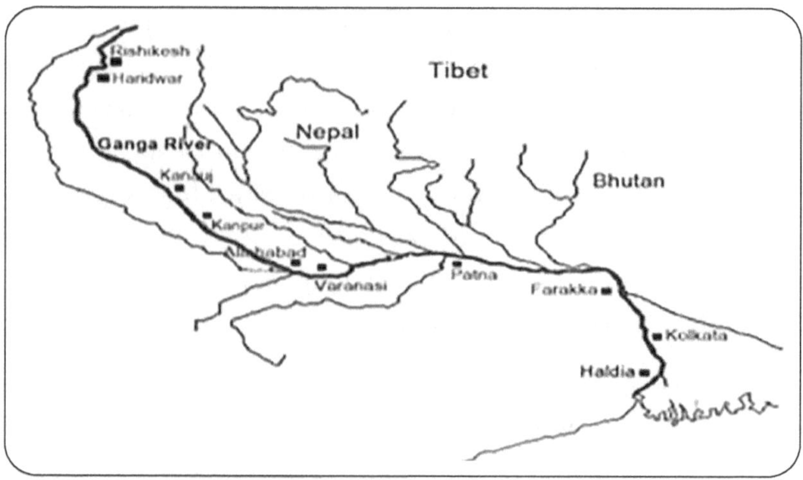


**Ganga River**

River banks are the cradles of all ancient civilisations. It is the societal refinements which started in the human settlements along the banks of rivers Sindhu, Nile, Euphrates-Tigris etc thousands of years ago, which paved the way for all the cultural, scientific and social advancements we see around us today. The Indian civilisation which even Alexander the great held in awe and veneration was spawned on the banks of River Ganga centuries before Christ. It was there that scriptures and Vedic theories, Vedic rites and philosophies evolved. So also, as the development of languages. It was working from the hermitages along the banks of Ganga that, our great sages created our epics as well as the astrological science, Ayurveda etc we use even today.

The greater part of the Indo-Gangetic Plains across which Ganga flows is the heartland of India. It is in this area that the successive civilizations from the Mauryan empire of Ashoka in the 3rd century BC to the Mughal Empire founded in the 16th century developed. Although, officially as well as popularly called Ganga in Hindi and other Indian languages, internationally this river is known as the 'Ganges'.

River Ganga is not just another river for most Indians. From time immemorial, River Ganga has been revered as a holy river in Hinduism. For many, Ganga is divine, and a medium to attain salvation. Many followers of Hindu, Budha, Sikh and Jain faiths believe that by dipping in Ganga, especially in Ganga at Kasi, they can wash away their sins. Not surprisingly, Ganga is also known as Papanashini and Vishnu Paadi. Jhanhvi, Mandakini, Bhageerathi etc are also the aliases of Ganga.

Ganga water is considered 'holy', and many people believe that it can cure diseases; though the rationalists pooh-pooh it. But, the truth is, Ganga water has some curative powers which other river waters don't have. Lending credence to this belief, way back in 1896, the British bacteriology expert Mr. Ernest Hanvury Hankin had discovered after extensive studies that Ganga water can destroy the germs/ bacteria/ microbes of many contagious diseases. In the nineteenth century, Cholera had a free run in India as an epidemic. It was discovered then that Cholera germs will be destroyed within three hours of coming in contact with Ganga water. Complementing this, the Malaria Centre at Delhi has found that mosquito larvae won't survive in Ganga water. Validating this, it is seen that especially in the regions upstream of Haridwar, mosquitos were not seen. Believers can take solace from these stories.

Lengthwise, at 2510 kilometres, Ganga with an average depth of 16 metres, is the fifteenth longest river in Asia and the thirty-ninth longest in the world. The river Bhagirathi is one of the two headstreams of River Ganga and is said to be the source stream of the Ganga. Bhagirathi River originates from the Gaumukh caves in Himani, near Gangotri. River Alaknanda originating from Badari Nadh is the second source stream of Ganga. Alaknanda, joined by its tributaries Dhauliganga river at Vishnuprayag, Nandakini river at Nandaprayag, Pindar River at Karnaprayag, and Mandakini River at Rudraprayag, meets the Bhagirathi River at Devprayag; and together they become officially River Ganga.

After that, many important Tributaries originating from the Himalayas as well as the plains join Ganga. They include Ramganga, Gomti, Ghaghara, Gandak, Kosi and Mahananda from the left bank, and Yamuna, Tamsa, Son, Punpun and Damodar from the right bank. In India, Ganga is the river with the highest number of tributaries. River Yamuna, at 1376 km in length, is thes longest among them. Ganga's second longest tributary is Ghagara; known also as Sarayu which, though second in length, is the largest as far as capacity is concerned. River Sarayu is known as the sorrow of India. As per legend, it was on the bank of this river that King Dashradh's arrow accidentally killed Shravan Kumar, the son of the blind hermits, and the hermits cursed the king that he too will die from the sorrow of the loss of a son. Also, it was into the depth of this river that Lord Sri Rama disappeared after the completion of his mission as the seventh incarnation.

As the tributaries from the Himalayas and those from the Indian Peninsula join Ganga, it will turn into almost an ocean. At Farakka in West Bengal, the river divides into two arms namely; Bhagirathi which flows through West Bengal, and the Padma which flows into Bangladesh where it joins Brahmaputra (which is called Jamuna in Bangladesh) near Goalundo Ghat at a place called Charnpur. After that, Ganga merges with the Bay of Bengal. As Ganga passes from West Bengal into Bangladesh, several distributaries branch off to the south into the river's vast delta which is nothing but the seaward prolongation of sediment deposits from the Ganges and Brahmaputra River valleys. Though for most of its course, Ganga flows through Indian territory, its large delta in the Bengal area which it shares with the Brahmaputra river, lies mostly in Bangladesh.

Sundarbans is a mangrove area in the delta formed by the confluence of Padma, Brahmaputra and Meghna Rivers in the Bay of Bengal. It spans the area from the Baleswar river in Bangladesh's division of Khulna to the

Hooghly River in India's State of West Bengal. The Sundarbans mangrove forest, at 105000 sq. km, is one of the largest of its kind in the world. This area is intersected by a complex network of tidal waterways, mudflats and small islands of salt-tolerant mangrove forests, and presents an excellent example of ongoing ecological processes. The area is known for its wide range of fauna, including 260 varieties of birds, the Bengal tiger, and other threatened species such as the estuarine crocodile and the Indian python.

Taking a dip in Ganga was a long cherished ambition spawned in me as a teenager while performing the last rites of my father. My first meeting with Ganga is still fresh in my mind. It was from the Howrah Bridge in Hooghly, a distributary of Ganga that I got to see her for the first time; though only from a distance, when I passed through Calcutta (now renamed as Kolkata) while on an all-India tour in my final year in college. My first serious opportunity to fulfil my wish came during my post-graduation days at Kolkata when our professor Mr. Nibesh Chowdhary took us to the river on the ferry near the famous Kalighat temple to show us the extent of pollution in the river. This time I could get close enough to take a dip, but was put off seeing its filthy condition. Another opportunity to take a bath in Ganga came my way during my visit to a water treatment plant in Ganga, but I was dissuaded from fulfilling my wish due to the high currents. My misfortune followed me during my next visit also which came after three months. This time, though it was summer, due to the melting of snow in the Himalayas, the river was flooded beyond the danger mark preventing me from getting into the water. Incidentally, on this visit, I was staying at a bungalow where Mr. Dalhousie, a viceroy of British India once stayed.

But, I couldn't be denied for ever. During those days as a student in my post-graduation course, I didn't even imagine that one day, I will be getting the opportunity to get involved with this epic river much more intimately. That came ten years later when I was posted as an engineer in the Ganga Action Plan. Thus, I had the good fortune to work as a frontline soldier on this prestigious divine mission.

It was in Kanpur that many industrial effluent treatment plants of Ganga Action Plan were located. During my official visits to the plants, I used to go up to the banks of the river. The nauseating sight of the multi-coloured murky water carrying so much of filth and even carcases of animals was a highly distressing one. This raised in my mind questions on the sanctity of the belief that dipping in this water will clean up one's soul. With that, I consigned to the back burner, my desire of taking a bath in Ganga.

Ganga's flow through the hill ranges is pristine with less human meddling, but that is not the case when she reaches the plains where the river is subjected to extreme abuse and pollution. The main culprits were, the chemical and organic discharges from the factories along its banks, the garbage – even sewerage lines - from households, and the most despicable practice of dumping partially burnt corpses into the river from the cremation grounds along the banks. This they did to save on firewood. See, what Ganga is getting in return for providing the livelihood for millions since time immemorial.

According to legend, King Bhagirath observed monumental penance facing every conceivable hardship for years and years to bring down Ganga from heaven to earth to enable his ancestors to attain salvation. King Bhagirath had to work so hard at it that, the term 'Bhagirath Efforts' got established in Indian vernacular languages as the last word for any super human effort. I am sure, had he had any inkling of what was ultimately going to happen to this holy river at the hands of humans, King Bhagirath would have left the souls of his ancestors to wander in the wilderness rather than bringing River Ganga down for them to attain salvation. To get Ganga restored into her old glory, virtually, nothing less than another 'Bhagirath effort' would be needed.

Sadly, in the early eighties, River Ganga was leading the list of the most polluted rivers in the world. Due to the pollution in Ganga, some 140 types of fish and 50 varieties of animals are facing extinction. Realising the urgent need for taking corrective action, on the 5th of February 1985, the then Prime Minister Mr. Rajeev Gandhi kicked off the Ganga Action Plan (GAP). Incidentally, though it was Mrs. Gandhi who mooted this idea, it was Mr. Rajiv Gandhi who was destined to get it rolling after Mrs. Gandhi fell to the bullets of her security guards.

Mr. Rajeev Gandhi made a remarkable speech on the occasion of the launch of that initiative. His words were "We will protect the sanctity of Ganga; no matter what it takes. In the olden days, India was synonymous with Ganga. That Ganga has become the most polluted in the modern days. We shouldn't waste any time in restoring Ganga to her lost glory."

The objective of the Ganga Action Plan was to bring down the level of pollution in Ganga by 75% of what it was. But, cleansing Ganga, with its financial, political and social implications, was too complex for an early solution. The job involved the coordination of various stakeholders like the ministry of environment, ministry of industry, Central Pollution Control Board, State Pollution Control Boards of U.P, Bihar, West Bengal and Uttarakhand, the Municipal Corporations of Kanpur and Patna, the National Textile Corporation, leather industry, jute mills etc. Thus, some of the pollution came within the domain of the civic bodies, and some others in the domain of the ministry of industries. The unholy nexus between some people who mattered in the political/ official fields and the offenders was another headwind faced by GAP. So, cleansing Ganga was easier said, than done.

As a consultant of the Ganga Action Plan, I was assigned to the group in charge of controlling the pollution from industrial units in Kanpur area. Among all the industrial units polluting River Ganga, the main offenders were the textile mills 'Elgin' and 'Muer ' who had their origins during the British rule, and a leather factory by name 'The Imperial Tannery.' They all were located in Kanpur. My job was to install the effluent treatment plants in these three factories on a turn-key basis. I could execute this project; thanks to the able support from organisations like Tata Consultancy Services. Thus, Kanpur provided me with the opportunity to accomplish one of the most creditable achievements in my life.

I remember a funny incident which occurred during this time. One day I left my house a bit early to a site where effluent treatment plant was under construction. As I was nearing the gate, I could hear a commotion. Sounded like slogan shouting. I could hear my name Ramachandran mentioned amidst the melee. I was scared. When we called it a day yesterday evening, everything was fine, with no labour issues whatsoever. Have the workers started an agitation on some trivial issues as they do in Kerala, I wondered. Nervously I went in. To my great relief, I found that the workers were starting their day with the prayer "Jai Ramchandraji ke jay". They usually start the work with this slogan, paraising Sri Rama.

Even though the Ganga Action Plan started in the right earnest, it could achieve only limited success. Then, in the year 2014, on the occasion of taking the oath, Prime Minister Mr. Narendra Modi declared that he will purify Ganga. For that, a master plan named 'Namami Ganga' was made. The government of Germany has given a loan of 120 million euros towards this project. The first stage of this project is since completed. As a result, the pollution in Varanasi and surrounding areas has reduced considerably.

Further on the topic of rejuvenation of River Ganga, in 2015, the authorities had introduced a pilot afforestation program as part of the National Mission for Clean Ganga (NMCG) – a Central scheme to rejuvenate the ailing Ganga. Encouraged by the result of this program, On March 14 2022, the Union environment ministry unveiled a plan to rejuvenate 13 major rivers in India using "forestry interventions". A major thrust of the plan is to afforest river banks.

The thirteen rivers that will form part of the rejuvenation project include:

1. Himalayan Rivers: Jhelum, Chenab, Ravi, Beas, Sutlej, Yamuna, and Brahmaputra.

2. Deccan or Peninsular Rivers: Narmada, Godavari, Mahanadi, Krishna, & Kavery.

3. Inland drained Category River: Luni.

These 13 rivers cover nearly 57.45% of India's geographical area, and they together run for 42,830 km, and drain more than half of India's geographical area.

The rationale to use "forestry interventions" to rejuvenate the rivers is that, riverbank afforestation will recharge groundwater and ensure perennial flow. The project proposes distributing saplings to farmers, planting fruit- and timber-producing trees, constructing staggered contour trenches for soil and water conservation, promoting ecotourism, etc. This will increase forest cover, carbon sequestration and groundwater recharging; reduce sedimentation and create jobs, the planners claim.

## About the Project

Indian Council of Forestry Research and Education (ICFRE) prepared the detailed project reports (DPRs) of the 13 rivers selected for rejuvenation. The cost of the project is projected to be 19,342.62 crores, and will take five years for implemention. This project could increase India's forest cover by up to 7,417 square kilometers. The riparian forests function as the natural buffers and biofilters, thereby supplementing the self-purification process of rivers. These forests will create carbon sinks, as they absorb atmospheric carbon dioxide; thereby helping India in meeting the carbon sequestration goals. According to the DPRs, these riparian forests have the potential to sequester 50.21 million tonnes of $CO_2$ equivalent after 10 years, while after 20 years they are expected to sequester 74.76 million tonnes of $CO_2$e. $CO_2$ equivalent means Carbon dioxide ($CO_2$) or any other GHG having the same global warming potential as $CO_2$.

India had pledged to create a carbon sink of 2.5 to 3 billion tonnes of $CO_2$ by 2030. In 2015, as a part of the Bonn Challenge, India has pledged to restore 5 million ha of degraded land by 2030. So, in addition to rejuvenating the rivers, this 13 rivers rejuvenation project will support India's international commitments under the Paris Agreement, the UN Convention to Combat Desertification and the Sustainable Development

Goals, the Union government hopes. So, it is many birds in one stone. However, it has also to be admitted that there are many people who are sceptical about the success of these grandiose plans.

Coming back to my interactions with River Ganga, when I visited Ganga again at Haridwar and Rishikesh after another fifteen years of my first visit, I was welcomed by a Ganga flowing serenely with crystal clear water rekindling my desire to take a bath in Ganga. The water level was low, not too cold, and almost standstill. It couldn't get better than this, I was sure. I dipped and dived in the river to my heart's content. That was a day I will never forget. Not only because of my religious sentiments; but also remembering that I too had a role in resurrecting this great river. I consider it as one of my most creditable legacies to my descendants.

Came dusk time at Haridwar, the floating chirags (small oil lamps, the size of a half coconut shell) let loose by the devotees, started drifting on Ganga. Those chirags and their oscillating reflections on water looked like a thousand stars fallen from the skies.

My onward journey from Rishikesh to Devaprayag, and from there to Badrinath was by road along the river banks. The road along the river bank being at a much higher level than the river, the travel by road was nerve-wracking; but also awe-inspiring. The village along the way where river Bhageerathi flows is still fresh in my memory. On one side of it, are the Neelakanda Mountains shining majestically in the sunlight. Around sixty degrees away is the Vyasa Cave, the abode of the great sage Veda-Vyasa who created the epics. Another sixty degrees away is the Badrinath temple which came into being due to the efforts of Adi Shankara. A stone's throw away flows River Bhageerathi. Who can leave such a place in a hurry?

Badrinath remains active only for six months a year; and for the next six months, the town, including the temple, hibernates due to extreme cold and snowfall. Legend has it that this place got this name because once God Vishnu sat on penance under a 'Badri' tree here.

Out of the 2510 km length of Ganga, 1450 km is flowing through Uttar Pradesh. The region where Ganga flows is very fertile. This area is known as the Northern Great Plains of india. Some 40 crore people live in the Ganga river basin. Ganga is the main lifeline to people living along its course. This river provides drinking water in addition to meeting at least 50% of the farming requirements of eight States of India. The Ganga River basin is around 26% of the total river basins in India. With its catchment area spread over entire Central India, Ganga can also boast of the largest catchment area among all Indian rivers. On November 4, 2008, Ganga was declared the National River of India.

Coming to the cities along the banks of Ganga, the important ones are Badarinadh, Deva Prayag, Rishikesh, Haridwar, Allahabad, Aligad, Kanpur, Meerut, Ganaj, Mirzapur, Hajipur, Varanasi, Patna, Farakka etc. Among them, Kanpur is the largest. Kanpur also is the financial and industrial capital of Uttar Pradesh. The city of Kanauj, known as the 'Perfume Capital of India' is near Kanpur. This place is also known as a centre for the tobacco trade. The Indian Institute of Technology at Kanpur is a renowned institution. I had the opportunity to execute some projects associated with the scientists of this Institute. There are many Buddhist institutions also here. Kanpur was an important military base during British rule. Kanpur also grew as an important centre for the leather and textile industries. Due to the large concentration of textile mills here, Kanpur is also called the Manchester of North India. Population-wise, Kanpur is the 12th largest city in India.

From Kanpur, Ganga reaches Allahabad. Earlier, this place was known as Prayag. It is at Allahabad that the River Yamuna is joining Ganga. The holy place Triveni Sangamam where the mystic subterranean River Saraswati supposedly joins Ganga and Yamuna is also at Allahabad.

Mirzapur in Uttar Pradesh has a distinction. That is, the Indian Standard Time is set on the longitude of Mirzapur which is 82 degrees and 32 minutes. Between Gujarat on the western side and Arunachal Pradesh on the eastern end of India, technically, there is a time difference of two hours. That is why the time at Mirzapur which is midway between the two ends of India is accepted as the Indian time. There is a 1000 kg heavy clock in Mirzapur. Its case is carved out from a single block of granite.

While talking about the cities in the context of Ganga, the name which comes to everyone's mind is the modern-day Banaras; previously known as Varanasi or Kasi. This is an epic city; the city of silk, a city of knowledge present in many legends. Kasi is one of the oldest cities in the world. It was at Saranadh, some ten kilometres away from Kasi that Bhagawan Sri Buddh was supposed to have given his most important discourse. Not surprisingly, Banaras is a pilgrim centre for Buddhists and Jains. The birthplace of their eleventh incarnation Shreyanasnadh is close to Saranadh. People of Vashnavite and Saivaite sects co-exist here peacefully. Varanasi is also rich in cultural fields like music and dance. World famous musicians Pandit Ravishankar and Ustad Bismillah Khan belong to this place. Not surprisingly, because this city is the venue for many music events; thus providing the ideal setting for the growth of musicians. Banaras is also known for the Banaras Hindu University which is famous for its contribution to the field of Ayurveda. Banaras, as everyone knows, is also known for its silk sarees. Banaras can also boast of its rose flower essence business. It is said that rose essence costs up to one and a half lakh rupees a litre in the international market.

In Bihar also, Ganga is flowing caressing many historically important places. River Sone, joining Ganga at Patna, is the southernmost tributary of Ganga. Its origin is at the Amarkhandak Plato in the State of Madhya Pradesh. River Sone has a tributary by the name Rihand. It is in River Rihand that the Govind Vallabh Panth dam is built. Patna, the capital of Bihar is on the banks of Sone. According to the epics, Patna was the capital of Magadha, the kingdom of Jerasandhan. During the Mourya reign, this city was known as Pataliputra. There are many places of worship for Buddhists, Hindus and Jains in this city. The Nalanda University of olden days is also here. Scholars like Aryabhatta, Chanakya, Vatsyayan etc are the sons of Patna. Bhagalpur on the bank of Ganga in Bihar is a highly fertile area. Bhagalpur was the capital of the kingdom 'Anga' which Karna ruled as per the epic Mahabharatha. The famous Manasadevi temple is also here.

Hajipur was the capital of the Vysali dynasty. With River Ghandak flowing on its western side, and River Ganga flowing on its southern side, Hajipur is a very beautiful place. The world-famous Sonapur Cattle Fair and Sonapur Music Festival are held here. Needless to say, the Vysali festival also is held here. This place also boasts of a pillar which was said to be visited by Buddha.

It is in Jabalpur that the famous Locomotive station of Indian Railways is located. In 1862, it was the British people who started the Railway Institute here. It is also believed that Jabalpur is the birthplace of the organisation Anandamarg, which caught the headlines for all the wrong reasons a few years back. Jabalpur is also famous for Tantric Yoga.

It is on the banks of Ganga at Haridwar and Prayagraj that, the world-famous Kumbhamela takes place. Kumbhamela, also held at Ujjain on the banks of the Sipra river, a tributary of the Chambal River in Madhya Pradesh is a Hindu pilgrimage confluence occurring once in twelve years. Up to 10 crore devotees are known to attend Kumbhamela. The half-Kumbhamela, its scaled down version takes place once in six years.

From Bihar, Ganga enters Bengal. Kolkata city is on the banks of River Hooghly which is a distributary of Ganga. Kolkata was the capital of British India. Kolkata has since extended to Saltlake city which is a satellite city of Kolkata. The first metro rail in India was started at Kolkata in 1984. The oldest tram service in Asia is also here. Most of the old buildings in Kolkata are built in Victorian architecture. There are fourteen universities in Kolkata. Nobel laureates Amartya Sen, CV Raman and of course Rabindra Nath Tagore are the products of the universities of Kolkata. One can say, Kolkata is the cultural capital of India.

The Kali idols in the Kalighat temple in Kolkata have some unique features. The Sanctum sanctorum of this temple is known as Shashti. There are three stones installed there. They are Shashti, Sheetala and Mangala

Chandi. The priests of this temple are all women. Kolkata is also famous for Durga Pooja and Saraswati pooja.

To me, the most enlivening place in Kolkata is the Shantiniketan. I have visited that place many times during my days in Kolkata. It is a three-hour train ride from Kolkata. The very ambience of this place, the surroundings rekindling memories of Tagore etc are rejuvenating. One can see many scholars from different parts of India engaged in their vocations there.

There are four important bridges in Hoogly. They are, the Ravindra Sethu, Vivekananda Sethu, Vidyasagar Sethu, and Nivedita Sethu. The Ravindra Sethu was formerly known as Howrah Bridge. The longest bridge in Ganga is the Mahatma Gandhi Sethu in Patna, Bihar. The Howrah Railway Station near the Howrah bridge built during the British rule is one of the most important railway stations in India.

The Ganga River basin is 1086000 sq. km in area. River Ganga's sources of water are rain, tributaries and melting snow. From July to October, this area receives the rain brought in by the southwest monsoon. The average rainfall in the western end of the river basin is 760mm, and on the eastern side, 2290mm. The rainfall in the central region of the river basin lying mostly in Bihar is 1000 to 1500mm, and in the delta region, it is 1500 to 2500mm. The catchment areas of River Ganga receive one million cubic metres of rainwater per sq. km on an average. 30% of it is calculated to be lost through evaporation. 20% get absorbed into the soil. The balance 50% utilisation is expected. In the warm months from April to June, the river receives water from the melting snow of the Himalaya mountains. The contribution of the tributaries to Ganga is estimated at 525 billion cubic metres. The hydroelectric potential of Ganga and its tributaries at around 51700 to 128700 MW is huge. 40% of it is in India.

The Ganga – Yamuna area was a forest at one time. Wild elephants, bison, rhinos, lions, tigers etc roamed freely there till the 17th century. But, nowadays there are only foxes, wolves, and the like there. The only exception is the Sunderbans area at the seafront where one can see Bengal tigers, crocs and marsh deer.

Scientists have discovered that River Ganga is becoming shallower, and is also changing its course. In Haridwar, it is reported that Ganga has changed track by up to 500 metres. Over the years, Ganga has shifted up to two and a half kilometres at some places in Bihar.

The inhabitants of the Ganga basin are a mixed race, speaking Dravidian or Austro-Asiatic languages. Later, people speaking Indo-Aryan languages joined them. Still, later, people from Turkey, Mangolia, Persia, Arab countries etc came from the west and got mixed with them. Especially in Bengal, people speaking Austro-Asiatic, Indo-Aryan, and Tibeto-Burmese languages got integrated with the natives.

The total length of national waterways in River Ganga is 1620 km. I have travelled on ferry service from Allahabad to Haldia. This service touched Patna on the way. In the olden days, Ganga and its tributaries were important waterways for transportation. By the 19th century, waterways in Ganga became the main arteries of transportation. Now, one can see large steamers in Ganga. I have seen huge steamboats in Hubli transporting jute bundles. They were similar to the boats I had seen on River Mississippi in America. But, with the advent of railways by the middle of the nineteenth century, the glorious days of water transportation came to an end. Even so, West Bengal and Bangladesh still depend a lot on water transportation for the movement of jute, tea, and other agricultural products. Chalna, Khulna, Barisal, Chandpur, Narayanganj, Golundo Ghat, Siraj Ganj, Bhairab Bazar, and Fenjuganj in Bangladesh and Kolkata, Golpara, Dhuburi, Dibrugarh in India etc are the major river ports. With the partition of India in 1947, East Pakistan came into being; and in 1971, it became Bangladesh. This had far-reaching consequences in many areas including water transportation. Among them are the hindrances faced in the transportation of goods from Assam to Kolkata.

## Ganga – Kaveri Link Master Plan

There was a brilliant Civil Engineer by the name of Mr. K.L. Rao in the central ministry during the years 1963 - 73. He has authored many textbooks followed in Engineering Colleges. Mr. Rao was the brain behind the National Water Policy. Aimed at the optimum utilisation of our water resources, he introduced to the National Water and Power Commission, the idea of the National Water Grid. This plan divided India into four zones. The southern part of India is relatively water-starved. As a solution for this, the National Water Grid envisaged bringing water from the Ganga basin in the north, to the Kaveri basin in the south. Some 1700 cum/sec water was to be diverted through the Ganga – Kaveri link canal this way.

This is a highly ambitious, gargantuan project which when implemented would change the economic, and social landscape of India. The plan is also to have to have a waterway starting at Patna in Bihar, and ending at Kallanai in Tamil Nadu. This 2640 km long canal is to link rivers Sone, Narmada, Tapti, Godavari, Krishna, Kaveri etc. With this, the perennial water shortage problem of the Deccan Plateau, as well as places like Bijapur and Gulbarga in Karnataka, and places in Andhra Pradesh and Telangana would disappear, it is hoped. The project, in addition to the development of agriculture, is expected to boost employment, industrialisation, tourism etc also on an unprecedented scale. The possibilities are mindboggling. But, so too are the challenges – technical, social, environmental, and financial – involved in its execution. So, when and how this dream will materialise, is hard to say.

Ganga is an emotion, and passion of the Indians. It is intertwined with the cultural and social history of the country for thousands of years. The legend behind the origin of this river, that of King Bhagirath refusing to give up despite facing countless hardships to ultimately succeed in bringing down Ganga to earth is giving mankind the very valuable lesson of life 'Perseverance Is the Key to Success'. Ganga is also the heroine in the epic Mahabharata extolling the duty of a son to his father. In that story, Bhishma, the son of Ganga voluntarily embraced eternal celibacy, forgoing the cardinal pleasure to fulfil the desires of his father.

Ganga is flowing… From the heaven, she first landed on the mane of Siva in the Himalayas, then proceeded to caress Kailas on her way to pay obeisance to Narayanan at Badrinath, and further flowed down to Kasi where she was servile to Viswanath, while all along providing the ideal settings for the creation of our epics; as well as our cultural evolution. She is flowing……, passing Magadha, Mourya, Anga, Kasi, Kosala and Vanga paying homage to Gautham Buddh to Adi Shankara, and providing for millions tirelessly.

Like Gangaputhra Bhishma, I too had lost my mother early in life. So, Ganga is mother for me; the mother who embraces me with her waves of love every time I go to her. She is a mother not only to me; but also to countless other living beings. My only prayer to my countrymen is, please spare her from further mindless abuse.

Dear mother, I submit myself at your holy feet. Bless me.

# SABARMATI

## The Soothing Caress of Holy Chants

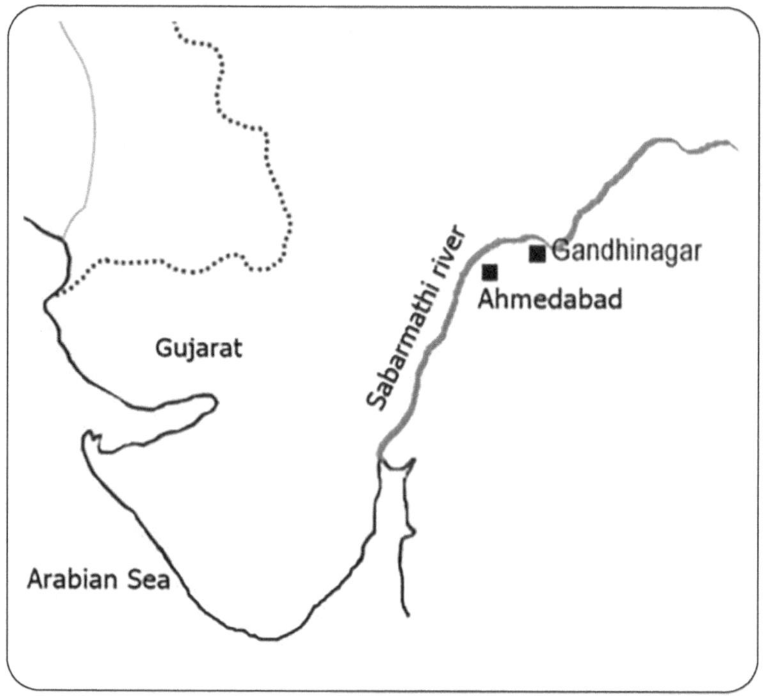


**Sabarmati River**

Most of the rivers in India are streaming down from the mountains. They all have some role in the Indian epics, and even connections with the gods or goddesses to boast of. But, there is one river which quietly flows through the soil of India as well as through the minds of Indians in absolute humility.

What that river is telling us is not the horror stories of wars and bloodshed which are the hallmarks of most of the epics; but, that of peace, tolerance and love. What reflects in its serene waters is not the multi-coloured godly images, but the withered figure of a half-naked Indian. The waves in this river are chanting not hymns praising gods; but, the prayer 'Oh God, give everyone a righteous mind'.

What the banks of this river facilitated for the Indians is neither the scriptures nor Vedic philosophies like the banks of Ganga did, nor the histories of invasions and subjugations as the banks of Sindhu did. Perhaps, in some ways, more than any other river, this river is the sacred river of India in the true sense of the term. Because it is the banks of this river which goaded Mahatma Gandhi into strategizing his freedom struggle based on the principles of non-violence. Thus, this river provided the ideal settings for the liberation of this country from the yokes of slavery. 'Sabarmati' is the name of that river.

Yes. River Sabarmati. She is not among the top rankers in length, size or any other parameters in comparison with the other rivers of India. Nevertheless, with her association with Mahatma Gandhi, she has earned a unique place for herself not only among the rivers in India, but in the whole world.

River Sabarmati is only 371 km long. Though this river is taking birth in a lake near Tepur in the Aravalli hill ranges of the Udaipur district of Rajasthan, logging 323 km in Gujarat, most of her flow till it joins the Arabian sea at the Gulf of Cambay is through her foster State Gujarat. The tributaries of River Sabarmati on its right side are Sei, Siri and Dhamni; and on the left side Wakal, Harnav, Hathmati, Khari and Watrak. Wakal and Sei also originate from the Aravalli hill range as River Sabarmati. As per the Gujarati folklore, River Sabarmati was a part of River Ganga which came along with Lord Sri Parameswaran when he came from the Kailas Mountains to Prabhasa Theertha.

Koteshwar Mahadev Temple, Shree Balamurugan Temple, and Shree Swaminarayan Mandir are the best known temples on the banks of River

Sabarmati. Somanadh temple, one of the most renowned Saivite temples in India, is also in Gujarat. This temple has been a target of repeated attacks by invaders. Ahmedabad, the financial capital of Gujarat, and Gandhinagar, the state capital of Gujarat, are on the banks of Sabarmati. The architecture of the city of Ahmedabad is highly impressive. It is said that the city of Ahmedabad was built by Sulthan Ahmed Shah in the year 1411. Vapi is another important town on the banks of River Sabarmati. This place is also known for diamond processing. Daman, the Indian territory under Portuguese rule till a few decades ago, is near Vapi.

An interesting feature of the River Sabarmati is that, while it gets its fame as the cradle of the four pillars of Gandhian philosophies - Satyagraha, Sarvodaya, Non-violence and Truth, the river, in its earlier days, had witnessed a lot of violence and bloodsheds due to the invasions as well as from battles between local kingdoms. But, the present identity of the river as one synonymous with peace is confirming to the world that, the ultimate victory is for peace.

There are many dams on River Sabarmati and its tributaries. The biggest among them is Dharoy, in the Mehsana district, built-in 1978. Dams Hanmati, Harnav and Guhay are constructed in the tributaries on the upstream side; and Meshwo reservoir, Meshwo pick-up weir, Masam Dam and Vastrok dam are in the tributaries on the downstream side.

It was in 1987 when I reached Ahmedabad in connection with my environment-related official assignment that I visited the shores of River Sabarmati for the first time. Though my job was to conduct the 'environment assessment' for Punjab National Bank, my mind was more on using this trip to visit the Sabarmati Ashram. So, I sounded this idea upfront to Mr. Harshendu Patel who received me at the airport, and he agreed to squeeze it into my itinerary. Mr. Patel far exceeded my expectation when I found the very next morning that, the first item in my day's program was a visit to the Sabarmati Ashram edging out the previously confirmed environment assessment. Perhaps, Mr. Patel was smart. He could have sensed that, once he can quell my fancy for the Ashram, I will be able to give all my attention to his audit.

There, on the bank of the serenely flowing Sabarmati, I got the first look at the Ashram of the great Mahatma. In the hustles of the breeze, as it skimmed the waves of the river, I could hear the 'Raghupati Raghava Rajaram' chants. Standing in those surroundings, I experienced an emotion unfamiliar and beyond words. In front of me was there Gandhi in his frail body, but with a steely resolve in his eyes, squatting on the floor with a rundown charka (portable, hand-made yarn spinning wheel). Was this the man who, without taking any weapon, defeated the mighty British Empire which boasted of as a country where the sun never sets? The epitome of simplicity; the sage who chanted "Hey Ram" as his last words even while a bullet pierced his heart. My eyes welled up. The feeling was beyond description in words. As I walked back to my car, I profusely thanked Mr. Patel for arranging this trip.

After this, during the past many years, I have visited Gujarat umpteen numbers of times. Every time, I saw to it that, I stayed at Hotel Cama on the bank of River Sabarmati so that I could spend my free time at the Gandhi Memorial, and also relax in the sands on the river bank if the season permitted. For anyone with at least some basic knowledge of Indian History, Sabarmati Ashram is as sacred a place as a temple.

The story about the origin of Gandhi Ashram goes like this. Immediately on his return from South Africa, Gandhiji decided to put up an Ashram in Ahmedabad. To begin with, he purchased one-acre land on the riverbank from one Mr. Premchandbhai for Rs 2556/; and the Sabarmati Ashram came up there in 1917. As per legend, this was the same place where the Ashram of sage Dadhichi once stood.

Till 1930, Gandhiji and Kasturba lived here in their modest dwelling named Hruday Kunj. Acharya Vinoba Bhave, the most venerated among the legion of Gandhi disciples lived in the Vinoba Kudeer which was next to Hruday Kunj. The Sabarmati Ashram was sandwiched between a jail and a cremation ground. About this, Gandhiji used to comment in jest that, either of those two places is the ultimate destination where a Satyagrahi – activist could end up.

Now, the sprawling 36-acre property of the Ashram is almost a pilgrim centre. There is a painting of Dhandi March kept in the Ashram. It was from the Sabarmati Ashram that Gandhiji started the famous Salt Satyagraha. That day, on March 12, 1930, Gandhiji set out from the Ashram accompanied by 78 inmates. His destination was the coastal village of Dandi in Gujarat. It took 24 days to cover the 384 km distance to reach the sea coast of Dhandi. This Salt Satyagraha was organised in protest of the heavy taxation the British government imposed on salt. The British had also prohibited Indians from producing, storing or trading in salt. Gandhiji's movement was against this draconian law, and it snowballed into a mass movement beyond anybody's expectations kindling the spirit of nationalism in the minds of Indians. It shook the foundation of the British Empire.

The biggest attraction in Sabarmati of course, is Hrudaya Kunj, the modest abode of the Gandhis. It is modelled in line with the housing of the common man in the Gujarat villages. Anyone visiting this place will instantly feel the presence of the soul of Gandhiji there. The Charka, walking stick, and the spectacles which Gandhiji used are exhibited there. But, though I could gain access to this place and take some photos, for obvious reasons, this place is 'out of bounds' for ordinary visitors.

Another attraction there is the Gandhi Museum. The then Prime Minister Mr. Jawaharlal Nehru dedicated the Gandhi Museum to the nation on May 10, 1963. There are some 280 odd enlarged photographs of the rare moments in Gandhiji's life, and another 8 oil paintings of Gandhiji exhibited there. I have visited this place twice. The kind of mental peace one experiences as one steps into the precincts of Gandhi Ashram is beyond description. Personal belongings of Gandhi, like his footwear, clothes etc also are exhibited here.

In South India, there is a similar Gandh Museum in an old palace in Madurai in Tamil Nadu. This place also is well kept, and worth a visit. I had been to this museum also twice.

As I write this, a recent development which caught my attention comes to my mind. There is an activist group of the few left over Gandhians in Kozhikode - the rare breed of people still valuing the Gandhian principles in the modern world where corruption, violence and communal hatred rule the roost. These octogenarian's only wish in their sun-set years now is to construct a memorial for Gandhi in the small 12 cents property they own in Kozhikode. But, to realise it, first of all, the tenants of the building in that plot will have to vacate. That is a highly complicated issue considering the laws in force here in such matters. One will also have to reckon with the too complex building rules in Kerala.

But, moves are afoot to see it happening. Some time back, the famous journalist Mr. K.P. Vijayakumar approached me with a request to help them in organising this. I conveyed to him that due to the shift of my residence from Kozhikode to Ernakulum, I may not be the best-suited person to spearhead this; not to mention my advanced age and the plethora of health issues. Nevertheless, being convinced that the idea is a noble one, I am trying my best to do for it whatever I can. I feel, in this 12 cents plot, they can have an institution replicating some of the essential features of the Gandhi Ashram. I have already requested my friend and classmate Mr. R.K. Ramesh to prepare a suitable design. Mr. Ramesh has agreed to do it free of cost. Hopefully, this materialises sooner than later, and thus the lifelong dream of those breed of noble souls on the verge of extinction will come true.

Gandhiji is almost forgotten today. But, if someone takes a serious look at the country's social fabric, it is easy to find that the Gandhian principles are all the more relevant in today's materialistic world. Modern lifestyles, coupled with distorted moral, familial and civic values have pushed our younger generation to the path of intolerance and violence. Introducing them to Gandhian philosophy can do a lot in diverting them from this path of destruction. Intelligent use of new technologies and social media could facilitate this. From my personal experience, I can vouch that a visit to a Gandhi Memorial/ Museum during their formative years will make a difference in their mindsets. The very ambience of the Sabarmati Ashram, as well as the river banks, is capable of instilling the spirit of non-violence and patriotism in the minds of any Indian. Organising conducted tours to a Gandhi Museum - if not to the Sabarmati Ashram - at least once during the schooling years of every student as a part of the curriculum could be considered. To facilitate this, we can also think of having a Gandhi Museum in every State capital.

Once the threat from Covid-19 ebbs, I am hopeful of making another trip to the Gandhi Ashram. My dream is to take dips in the river and walk on the riverbank enveloped in the 'Raghupati Raghava Rajaram' chants in the mumbles of the breeze there. I leave everything to 'TIME' to decide.

We started off talking about River Sabarmati, but often found ourselves discussing Gandhi memories. Not surprising, considering that Mahatma Gandhi's life and River Sabarmati are inseparable. Every drop in River Sabarmati will have a Gandhi story to reminisce. I will even say that the nation owes it to River Sabarmati as much as to Gandhi for securing the independence.

Starting in the Aravalli hills and ending in the Arabian sea, River Sabarmati flows on and on, carrying with her the most cherished memories of the most eventful period in the history of this country.

# GODAVARI

## Poignant Memories of Sita Devi

**Godavari River**

Rivers always fascinated me. My earlier interactions with rivers were limited to frolicking in the small streams in my native village Kattoor in my pre-teens; and later, in River Karuvannur and River Chalakkudi a bit away from home as I grew older. However, my love for rivers became a passion after I got intimately closer to the Chaliyar river during my stint as the Regional Pollution Control Engineer at Kozhikode where I was besieged with the pollution problems of that river. And it blossomed further when destiny extended my association with rivers through projects related to

Ganga, Yamuna, Krishna, Godavari, Brahmaputra; and also with the Rhine, Thames, Mississippi, and River Jordan, River Saint Lawrence etc.

Interestingly, my love for rivers was mutual, it appeared. Because, there were some situations where it was almost like the rivers were creating reasons for me to visit them. On other occasions, I was forced to visit rivers accompanying friends on their insistence. My chance visit to River Godavari was one among them.

It was during my Bombay days that one day, Ms Susmita Iyengar, daughter of my friend called me up quite unexpectedly. She said "Uncle, mummy and I have to go to Nasik tomorrow for conducting a Pooja there. Daddy is not well. He has asked me to request your help. Could you please accompany us?"

Nasik, an old city on the banks of River Godavari is one of the major cities of the State of Maharashtra. It is a tourist destination, a holy city and an industrial hub, all rolled into one. The Kumbh Mela held on the banks of Godavari here is also a famous event. Millions of devotees participate in it. Also, Aurangabad, the home of Ajanta – Ellora caves is not far away from Nasik. These cave temples were crafted in granite in the period between the 2nd century BC and the 7th century AD. They are included among UNESCO's world heritage sites. Even though they are accepted as monuments of Buddhist lineage, one can identify Jain and Hindu influences also in them. Nasik was a place I was longing to see for quite some time. Now, that opportunity was knocking on my door.

I didn't have any unavoidable assignments for the next couple of days. So, I didn't have to think twice to reply to Susmita 'Done'.

Susmita sounded relieved hearing my reply. She added "Thank you, uncle. We have to leave early morning. We will come in our car."

As planned, Susmita and her mother picked me up in the early morning the next day, and we left for Nasik.

Susmita is a brilliant architect. She was a rank-holder from the famous J.J. School of Arts, and a post-graduate in Green Architecture from San Fransisco. She used to get many marriage proposals; but, for some reason, none of them fructified. Her worried grandparents consulted an astrologer who identified that some problems in the planetary positions are the ones responsible for this. The solution for it was to conduct some special pooja. Triyambakeswar temple in Nasik specialised in this. That was the reason behind their trip to Nasik.

We reached the house of the Tantric at Nasik by 8 in the morning.

"How long will it take for the pooja to complete?" I asked.

"Till noon, at least. If you want, you can take a tour of the city." The Tantric replied as if having read my mind.

I had no role in the pooja proceedings. So, no point in waiting here. I took the car and left.

Nasik is a place with a lot of importance from the Indian mythological point of view, starting with the very name of the city. As per legend, it was on the bank of Godavari at Nasik that Laxman chopped off the nose and boobs of Soorpanakha. The meaning of the word 'Nasika' is nose. As per the folklore, Nasik got this name from this incident. Triyambakeswar temple, Panchavadi, Sita cave etc near Nasik also are some of the places connected with our epics.

It was to the Triyambakeswar temple that I went first. In Brahmagiri, not far away from the spot where River Godavari starts, there is a big bathing ghat. And, at a small distance from there, is the famous Sita Cave, and then the Triyambakeswar temple. It is in this temple that one of the only twelve Jyothirlingams in the world is installed. The holy water of this temple is known as Amruthavarshini.

Talking about Panchavadi; according to Ramayana, Panchavadi is the place where Lord Sri Ram granted salvation to the five Gandharvas who became five Banyan trees due to the curse of Sage Agasthya. At this place, is the huge Sita Cave carved out in granite. There, the idols of Lord Ram, Sitadevi and Laxman are installed. The access to this place is through the 3 feet high cave mouth located among granite boulders. One will have to crawl to enter the cave.

I took a dip in River Godavari and walked to the Sita Cave. After waiting at the cave mouth for a few minutes to catch my breath, I somehow squeezed in through it. As I stood in the cave immersed in thoughts about the Ramayana story, the scene of Lord Sri Ram singlehandedly fighting the Kharabhooshans and their fourteen-thousand strong army of demons after leaving Sitadevi secure in this cave with Laxman guarding her came to my mind. The thought that I was standing in the same cave where Sitadevi sat trembling worried about her husband battling those demons gave me goosebumps.

On my way back from the Triyambakeswar temple, I witnessed an extraordinary scene. Some people were setting fire to a huge human statue wrapped in dried cow dung. My curiosity forced me to pull over and enquire with the people, what it was all about. They explained to me that this ritual is for the salvation of people who died in accidents. Ordinary poojas won't suffice for accident victims, they believe. Hence this special one, they clarified.

River Godavari is a holy river for the Hindus. They celebrate Godavari Pushkaram on its banks every twelve years. Taking dips in this river during the Pushkaram is considered as divine as dipping in Ganga, many believe. Due to this, Godavari is known as Southern Ganga. River Godavari is also known as Vrudha Ganga as some people believe that she is older than Ganga.

The epics also say that the River Godavari was previously known as Gowthami. The story behind it is that, once, the area south of the Vindhya Mountains faced severe drought. To save the flora and fauna from this drought, Sage Gowthama sat on penance to invoke the blessings of Sree Parameswar. As the fulfilment of the penance, conceding to the wishes of Sage Gotham, Sree Parameswar created a river. Since the river was born out of the efforts of Sage Gowthama, it came to be known by the name Gowthami adding a feminine hue to Gowthama. The story further adds that honouring the desire expressed by the Sage, Sree Parameswar settled down as Jyothirlingam at the starting point of the river. This is the Jyothirlingam in the famous Triyambakeswar temple, people believe.

The 1465 km long Godavari is the second longest river in India after Ganga. Like River Krishna, River Godavari also is originating in Maharashtra near the west coast of India. She could have joined the Arabian Sea by travelling just 380 km from her birthplace at Thrayambakeshwar; but, like River Krishna, she too chose to go 1465kms east to join the Bay of Bengal. In this process, River Godavari had to take the arduous route through three other States viz. Telangana, Andhra and Chhattisgarh.

It is very difficult to reach River Godavari's origin located between three mountains by name Brahmagiri, Neelagiri and Kaaligiri. They are supposed to represent Brahma, Vishnu and Sivan. From there, she streams down through the boulder-packed hillsides.

There are many tributaries for Godavari. Ban Ganga, Katwa, Sivana, Poorna, Indravati, Pranahita, Warda, Manjeera, Kinnerasani, Sileru, Sabari, Dharana, Nasardhi, Pravara, Singfana, Manyr etc are they. Among them, it is in the Indravati river that the famous Chitrakooda waterfall known as the Niagra of India is situated. Since the hue of the waterfall changes with the season, this waterfall is also called the waterfall which changes its colour like a chameleon.

It was in the Dandakam forests on the banks of River Godavari that some of the most critical events of the epic Ramayana took place. Events like Soorpanakha's misdemeanours to entice Lord Sri Ram provoking Laxman to chop off her nose and boobs as mentioned above apart, Lord Ram killing the Kharabhooshans, Mareechan the illusionist disguised as the golden deer fooling Sitadevi to come out of the safe confines of the 'Laxman Rekha', Ravan kidnapping Sitadevi as she breached the 'Laxman Rekha' etc, were staged in the Dandakam forests. This forest was believed to be an area between River Godavari and River Narmada; and included

Panchavadi. Legend has it that, this forest was a country ruled by King Dandan of the Ikshaku dynasty, but was transformed into a forest following the curse of Sage Shukra Maharshi.

Bidding goodbye to Panchavadi and Ramayana stories, River Godavari enters the Gangapur reservoir. It is from the Kashyap dam near here that the city of Nasik draws water. At 25 km away from Nasik, a stream called Darna joins Godavari. Further down, at Ahmednagar, a small river Pravara also joins her.

From Nanded, Godavari takes twists and turns to reach the Vishnupuri dam. This is one of the world's largest lift irrigation projects. From there, Godavari flows towards Bhadrachalam in Telangana. This also is a place of religious importance. Here, there is a beautiful temple built by a hermit by name Ramdas.

The next destination of River Godavari is Kanukurthi in the Nizamabad district. Here, she is joined by rivers Manjeera and Haridra. Another 12 km from there, with the water from Sriram Sagar dam also joining Godavari, her width increases substantially. From there, River Godavari flows to Rajamundry in Andhra Pradesh. The holy place Pattiseema is near here. There is an important Siva temple there. It is after praying in this temple that the devotees participated in the Godavari Pushkaram at Rajamundry. The road-rail bridge in Rajamundry is also famous as the longest one in Asia when it was built.

The River narrows down considerably as she passes through the mountainous regions in Andhra Pradesh, but regains its size as she reaches Polavaram. It is here that River Sabari joins River Godavari. The Arthur Cotton Dam is located here. After this, River Godavari splits into two - as Gowthami Godavari and Godavari. A while later, Gowthami splits as Vasishta and Nilaveru. Vasishta further splits into Vasishtam and Vaithanya, and flows into the Bay of Bengal.

There are many wildlife sanctuaries and bird sanctuaries in the Godavari river basin. The National gardens in Ettoornagaram, Gowtala, Indravati, and Kamgar Ghati are famous among them. The bird sanctuaries at Kawal, Kinnerasani, Kolleru, Nagsira, Paiganga and Papikonda attract a lot of tourists. There are many waterfalls in this river flowing through many mountainous regions. Bogatha, Duduma, Pochera, Chitrakooda, Kunrala, Sahasrakunda, Tiratgarh etc are they.

River Godavari is deficient in water except during the monsoon months. Still, she irrigates some 4,05000 hectares of land. This river mainly caters to the needs of the farmers in the Deccan Plato, aided by various dams. Gangapur dam, Jayakwadi dam, Vishnupuri barrage, Khatkar dam, Upper Vaidarna reservoir, Sriramsagar dam, Sir Arthur Cotton Barrage, etc are the major dams in River Godavari. The major hydroelectric power stations are, Upper Indravati, Matchkund, Balimela, Upper Sileru, Lower Sileru and Polavaram. Godavari Bridge, the Godavari arch bridge and the Havelock bridge are the important bridges in River Godavari.

Some 60 lakhs of people depend on the Godavari directly or indirectly in their daily lives. The major beneficiaries of River Godavari are the cities of Nasik, Nagpur, Wardhwa, Nanded, Chandrapur of Maharashtra, Bhadrachalam, Nizamabad, Ramagundam in Telangana, and Rajamundri and Narzapur in Andhra Pradesh.

Most of the rivers and riverbanks in India have some connections with Hinduism. Among the exceptions is the place called Paithan on the bank of River Godavari. This place is known as a pilgrim centre of Jains. Their Digambar Athisay temple is a famous one. Paithan is famous for sarees also. Traditionally, it is the Paithan sarees which the brides in Maharashtra wear for their weddings.

There is a place called Jake Wadia, a destination for migratory birds near Paithan. Even Siberian Cranes are spotted there. 250km from Aurangabad, there is a place called Nanded. Takht Sri Hazar Sahib, built over the place where Guru Gobind Singh, the spiritual leader of the Sikh people was cremated in the year 1708 is here. So, this place is an important pilgrim centre for the Sikhs.

Sadly, like most other rivers, River Godavari also is at the forefront when it comes to pollution. 18% of it is from industries. The rest come from domestic sources.

Talks are on regarding the linking of Godavari and the other rivers. But, this is not as easy an idea as many people think. For example, take the Mahanadi – Godavari link system. In reality, this is Mahanadi – Godavari – Krishna –Pennar – Kaveri – Vaigai project. This project envisaged a big dam at Manibhadra in Orissa', but that would submerge many villages there. So, the government of Orissa opposed it. On 3rd December 2014, a meeting was held to discuss this issue. After this, on June 4, 2015, they made another design of the Manibhadra dam restricting submergence of fewer places. After this, on September 29, 2015, they handed over the design to the National Institute of Hydrology, Roorkee for conducting simulation studies. On 3rd March 2017, the National Institute approved the model. But, in July 2018, the government of Orissa again suggested some changes. Thus, this is going back and forth; and a decision acceptable to all, is yet to emerge.

Linking rivers is of course a great idea benefitting many. As of now, many of our reservoirs are short of water while at the same time from elsewhere, a lot of water is flowing out into the sea. This is causing a lot of distress among the farmers; threatening even the food security program of the country. River linking will provide a lasting solution for all these.

------------------------------------

As I was walking through Panchavadi, immersed in thoughts about River Godavari, my phone rang. It was Susmita on the other end.

"Uncle, where are you? The pooja is over." She said.

So, it is time for me to rush back. I glanced at River Godavari. She is flowing struggling to make her way through the boulders lying scattered on the riverbed. Standing on the banks of River Godavari, I felt that the waves of the river were reciting the poems on Sitadevi. What Nasik, Godavari and

Panchavadi rekindled in me were the tales of the grief of Sita, which Sage Valmiki described in tears and blood.

I became pensive. I was standing at a place which had witnessed so many events central to our epic Ramayana. This is the place where the chopped-off nose and breasts of Soorpanakha fell. A small distance away from where I stood, I could see the 'Laxman Rekha' though drawn with paint by the temple people. It is believed that this is drawn in the same place where the original 'Laxman Rekha', that divine line, which Laxman drew for the protection of Sitadevi as he left his guard and went in search of Rama. It is on this soil that Mareechan fell to the Manavastra of Rama; but, only after succeeding in his mission to lure Sitadevi out of the Laxman Rekha for Ravan to kidnap her. Not far away is the place where Jadayu dropped dead when Ravan cut off her wings as the bird tried to intercept the Pushpak aircraft in which Ravan was flying to Lanka with the kidnapped Sitadevi. River Godavari was a mute witness to all these events; and much more.

As I walked to the car after giving a final look at the Sita Caves and the river, my mind said "'TIME' permitting, I will come again to spend even more time with you."

# MAHANADI

## Sorrow of the Kalinga Region

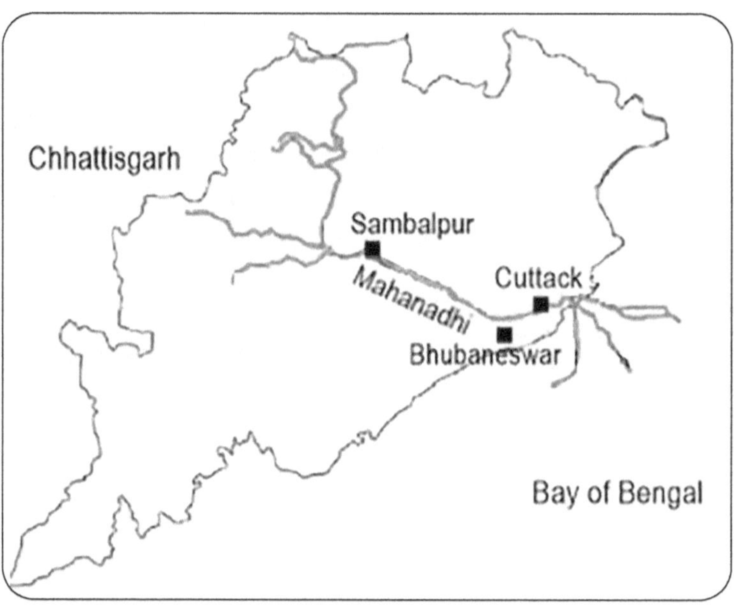



**Mahanadi River**

In the bygone era, on the east coast of the then greater Bharath which was then known as Jumbudweepam, there was a State called Ulkalam. Later, during the Mahabharatha period, this place came to be known as Kalinga. As per the legend, Bhanumati, wife of Duryodhan belonged to Kalinga, and Karn, king of Anga rajyam once defeated Kalinga in a war. However, none of these is the reason behind the historic importance of Kalinga.

Kalinga was the country which was instrumental in bringing about drastic changes in the life of Emperor Ashoka, the most powerful ruler Bharath has ever seen. Kalinga stood up against the invading forces of emperor Ashoka of the Mauryan Dynasty. What followed was a fierce battle which, of course, resulted in the victory of Ashoka, but at a heavy price of human lives. Moved by the sufferings the war inflicted on the defeated people, Ashoka renounced armed conquest; and instead adopted a policy called 'conquest by dharma'. The Emperor became an apostle of Buddhism not only in India; but, all over Asia. That Kalinga is known today as Odisha.

The 857 km long River Mahanadi's importance is that, it is the largest source of water for the States of Odisha and the neighbouring Chhattisgarh. The origin of this river which ends up in the Bay of Bengal is at the Shyamgi hill in the Sihava hill-ranges in the Raipur District of the Chhattisgarh State. There is a legend behind the origin of the River Mahanadi. It goes like this. Once, some hermits in an ashram decided to participate in the Kumbh Mela which is celebrated only every 12 years. But, it so happened that, at the start of this festival, the chief hermit, Sage Shrangi was on meditation. The other hermits waited for their chief to come out oee4xcxxf meditation so that they could take him also along. But, the sage was continuing in meditation even as the festival was nearing its conclusion. Since the other hermits didn't want to miss the rare Kumbha Mela, though reluctantly, they decided to rush to the festival leaving their chief behind.

After the festival, the hermits returned, collecting some holy water in their 'Kamandalu' (goglet bowl) for presenting to their chief. But, finding the sage still in meditation, they respectfully placed it at his feet taking care not to awaken him. A few days later, when the sage finally came out of his meditation and got up unaware of all these happenings, his foot accidentally toppled the Kamandalu, and the holy water from it began to flow. As the sage watched it in astonishment, the flow gradually became a river. Since this river originated from a Maha theertham (holy water), it got the name Mahanadi.

Sadly, River Mahanadi is also called 'the sorrow of Odisha' because Odisha faces lots of hardship due to the floods in this river. However, with the commissioning of the Hirakkud dam in 1957, the largest earth dam in the world, the havocs from the floods in Mahanadi have reduced. This dam is in the Sambalpur district of Odisha. However, it is said that this dam submerged some 50000 hectares of teak plantation leading to a big environmental issue in the later years when, as those teak trees began to rot, they released methane gas into the atmosphere in large quantities.

River Mahanadi is rather narrow in its first 80km which is in the northerly direction through Chhattisgarh. At the old Bilaspur in Chhattisgarh, the River Shiyonadh joins Mahanadi. From there, the river flows east towards Odisha to join the Hirakkud dam at Sambalpur. After this, she turns south for a stint with the Eastern Ghats, and then turns east to enter the Odisha plains near Cuttack. To protect the city of Cuttack from the floods in River Mahanadi, they have built a granite wall around the city. As if floods are not enough, Odisha has to endure surprise cyclones and torrential rains also.

After some kilometres of leaving Cuttack, a distributary by the name Katjodi branches out from River Mahanadi. Going further, the river undergoes more splits into several streams before finally merging with the Bay of Bengal.

Rivers Shiyonadh, Mand, Ib, Hasdeo, etc are the tributaries of River Mahanadi on its left side; and rivers Ong, Jonk and Telan on the right. River Shiyonadh, the largest among them was privatised once; but that was annulled later. The cities and towns on the banks of this river are Rajim, Sambalpur, Cuttack, Sonepur, Birmaharajpur, Subalaya, Kantilo, Boudh, Banki etc.

In Chhattisgarh, 15 medium-sized projects are planned in River Mahanadi. But, the Odisha government is raising objections against them. It is said that, due to the many dams in Chhattisgarh, scores of villages in Odisha are water-starved causing a lot of heartburns, especially among the farmers there. The water flow to the Hirakkud dam also is affected. In the year 2007, Odisha announced a water policy. In October 2017, the National Green Tribunal gave a verdict on the future construction of dams on River Mahanadi. In January 2018, the honourable Supreme Court gave the final judgment on it. The Central Water Commission also is trying to work out plans acceptable to both sides. Hopefully, with all these, the dispute between Chhattisgarh and Odisha in sharing the Mahanadi water will be a thing of the past. River water disputes are so complex that, they often defy solutions acceptable to all parties.

River Mahanadi has a drainage area of 82000 sq. km. Hirakkud dam, Ravishankar dam, Dudhava Reservoir, Sonder Reservoir and Dadula Reservoir are the major projects in River Mahanadi. It is the augmentation projects which are planned for the future. Apart from this, at Cuttack, they have planned a project called Mahanadi Riverfront Project under the Central Environment Department. However, the fact that the flow into the Hirakkud dam is progressively dwindling is a matter of big concern to all. Impact on agriculture apart, that has affected the production of electricity also.

There are 7 big irrigation projects, 119 medium-type lift irrigation projects and 82 small-size lift irrigation projects in River Mahanadi. Apart from that, there are 15000 water tanks installed at different places for household purposes. The government has earmarked Rs. 4000/- crores towards the development of ports in River Mahanadi.

The Mahanadi River basin, rich in deposits like lime, manganese, iron ore etc, is the 8th largest basin in the country having a total catchment area of 140000 sq. km with an average yearly rainfall of 1463mm. The basin receives about 90% of its rainfall during the monsoon season. This rainfall is uneven, and hence drought is prevalent in some districts. 14 districts in the basin are covered under the Drought Prone Area Programme.

Thus, sadly, River Mahanadi goes almost dry during summer; but also causes lots of flood damages during monsoon. Once the Mahanadi – Godavari link project is completed, that will address the drought and flooding problems to a large extent. For this, the Odisha government will have to construct a dam at Manibhadra in River Mahanadi. But, a dam at this place will have a big impact environmentally. So, they are working on various options to address the issue as explained in the chapter on River Godavari. Apart from that, they are also considering a dam at a place called Barmul, some 14 km upstream of Manibhadra. This will facilitate diverting some 4046 cu.m of water to the Godavari during the flooding months. The length of the link canal for this project is 842 km. But, this project will submerge 23000 hectares of land. Still, this project generating 240mw electricity and 125 million cu.m of drinking water apart from providing for irrigation, will be beneficial for the development of Odisha.

When it comes to pollution, River Mahanadi is no different from the other rivers in India. Wastewater from the townships along the banks is being freely let out into the river without any treatment worth its name. Farmers are complaining that the governments are allowing the uncontrolled use of water by the industries at the expense of agriculture. Compared to most other rivers, River Mahanadi used to carry a lot of silt. The problem of the accumulation of silt is another challenge.

## Puri Jagannadh Temple and Konark Sun Temple

It is near one of the many branches of River Mahanadi as she joins the Bay of Bengal that, Puri, the town which houses the Jagannadh Temple, a famous pilgrimage site is located. The Konark Sun Temple, a World Heritage Site is only a few kilometres away from Puri. Both Konark and Puri temples are also famous for their heritage in promoting music and dance.

I vividly remember my visits to the Puri Jagannadh Temple and the Konark Sun Temple during a 'music season' there. I had my friend and classmate Mr. Mahapatra for company. Mr. Mahapatra's expertise was not only in Engineering, but also in Odissi music and dance. He was only too happy to share with me his deep knowledge in those areas. As an icing on the cake, through Mr. Mahapatra, I could meet the doyen of Odissi music, Mr. Kelu Charan Mahapatra, and also enjoy a dance program by the famous Odissi danseuse Ms Sujata Mahapatra from a ring-side seat. After that experience, I have no hesitation in echoing the often heard comment in music circles that 'to appreciate the greatness and exclusivity of the Odissi singing and dancing, one has to watch the dance of Ms Sujata Mahapatra to the rendering of Mr. Kelu Charan Mahapatra.'

Odissi dance is acknowledged as a dance attributable to Odisha. Perhaps, only Odisha and Manipur can boast of having a dance form exclusive to a State. Odissi dancing is supposed to have originated at the Puri temple. Experts believe that this dance form is the classical form after merging certain features of the Devadasi dance 'Dasiyattam' with 'Kuchipudi'. Odissi dance form which is more than 700 years old, developed and became popular on the premises of the temples at Bhuvaneswar and Puri. Devadasis in Odisha are known as Maharis.

Coming to the Puri temple, it was King Ananthavarman of the Ganga dynasty in the 12th century AD that the decision to build the Puri Jagannadh temple was taken. In AD 1230, King Ananga Bhiman the 3rd dedicated his kingdom to the deity, and ruled the country as his servant - similar to what King Marthandavarma in Travancore did when he dedicated his kingdom to Sri Padmanabha, and ruled Travancore as Padmanabha dasan.

There is a big tower at the centre of the temple complex. Above that, there is a wheel. Devotees believe that this wheel is the 'Sudarsana Chakram' of Lord Vishnu. This tower is known as the white tower.

This temple has three main deities. They are; Krishnan, Balaraman and Subhadra. The 'Puri' festival in the month of Aashadam here attracts lakhs of devotees. In one of the rituals in this festival, they place the main idols in a chariot, and take them to a place called Gundicha Bari, some 4 km away. After a week, these idols are taken back to the temple. This ritual is to commemorate the shifting of Lord Krishna from Gokulam to Mathura. The chariot is 50 feet tall and 35 feet wide; and with 16 wheels, each wheel is more than 6 feet in diameter. It is pulled by the devotees themselves.

The Puri temple has a history of surviving many invasions also. From the Mughals to the Marathas to the East India Company, everyone who conquered Odisha established their control over this temple also.

Coming the world famous Konark Sun Temple, this temple is the ultimate example of Indian traditional Temple Architecture. It is said that the multi-level tower of this temple was appearing as a black coloured pagoda for the seafarers from their long-distance view, and hence came to be known as the Black Pagoda.

The Konark Sun Temple is equally – if not more - famous as the Puri Jagannadha temple. It is believed that the 'Konaditya' mentioned in the 'Brahmanda puranam' is this temple only. Built in the 13th century AD, Konark Sun Temple is designed in the shape of a big 100 feet tall chariot with seven horses. There are twelve sculpted wheels on either side of it. Each one of these wheels is a kind of sun-clock. It is said that, they can be used to find the time accurately. On the walls of the temple, one can see the figures of the characters of the epics carved out in granite. There are 2000 statue elephants around the temple. The sculptures of two lions stand as guards at the entrance.

Linking rivers was a dream of many from all walks of life since long. The mother of them all is a grand plan linking the 16 Himalayan rivers and 14 Peninsular rivers. Down south, the committee formed for the linking of River Mahanadi and River Godavari was headed by Mr. Sriram Vediyar. Permission for proceeding with this project was received on 25th February 2021. The plan is to finalise a report ensuring that Telangana and Andhra Pradesh use the Godavari water as allotted to them through the proposed Mahanadi-Godavari link canal.

The delta created by rivers Mahanadi, Baitharani and Bramini is one of the largest deltas in India. Spread between Chilikalagoon and Dhamara river bank, it is some 200 km long. That is, from Puri till Bhadrak. It is not unusual for people to migrate to the delta regions for farming and other occupations. Such migrations are on the increase in the delta region of River Mahanadi.

In the national anthem of India, Tagore has inserted the word 'Ulkalam'. This is the old name of Kalinga. In the epic Mahabharatha, there is a mention of Kalinga refusing to pay tax to the more powerful Magadha and Hastinapur kingdoms. Kalinga took this defiant stand believing that Magadha and Hastinapur won't be able to cross River Mahanadi to come over to Kalinga. That may be the reason why even emperor Ashoka who had no difficulty in conquering all the countries from Afghanistan to Nepal to Burma, had a hard time subduing Kalinga. But, it was not ecstasy but agony that the victory in that war gave to emperor Ashoka. The remorse ensuing from it transformed a blood-thirsty king into one following Buddhism adhering to the path of non-violence. One can say that the Kalinga war was instrumental in changing the course of Indian History.

Rivers are with pre-historic origins. They support life on this planet. So, at least for our own sake, we must resurrect them from the mindless pollution and abuse perpetrated on them by mankind through generations. But, for that, we have to first cleanse our minds of greed. Unless and until we realise that earth can't sustain any form of life without rivers, and also that the other living things on this planet have as much right on the rivers as us, the rivers will continue to be at the receiving end of the mindless violence at the hands of the mankind.

Yes. It is this realisation which can work as the change agent. The same realisation which transformed emperor Ashoka from a blood-thirsty invader to a pious Buddhist. So, let us hope, our attitude towards rivers undergoes a sea change, and our minds also transform into streams flowing with noble thoughts.

## Swot (Surface water and ocean topography)

The satellite named SWOT blasted off from California yesterday (12.16.22) and the satellite entered expected to orbit in space. This satellite is for learning about all major rivers in the world. SWOT satellite is working in collaboration with Canada and the UK.

Among the water resources in India, the satellite will conduct a special study of the Mahanadi and Pookot Lakes in Wayanad. I have two reasons to feel particularly happy about this mission. I studied at M.A College of Engineering Dr J Indu who studied in the same college is a scientist from India who is involved in this satellite mission. Similarly, the CWRDM in Kozhikode, where I worked as the Registrar for some time, is providing institutional support from India for the SWOT mission.

# NARMADA
## Favourite Daughter of the Vindhya Mountains

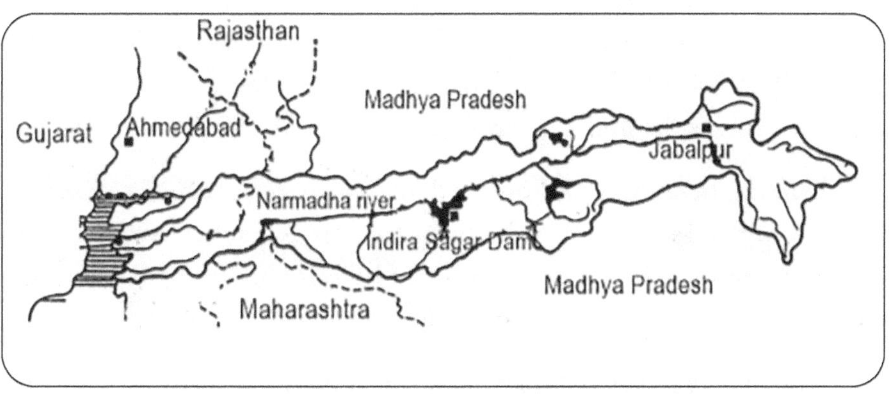

**Narmada River**

Who was the first in the world to construct a dam across a river? A very interesting question; but, in none of the search sites, there is a definite answer for it; except a guesswork that, maybe, the Egyptians, at around 2900 BC. However, there is a specific mention of that hero in the epic Valmiki Ramayana. According to it, King Karthaveeryarjuna, the king of Haihayas had built a dam across a river to enable him and his hundreds of wives to take baths to their heart's content. As if to lend further credence to this claim, the story adds that it is in this same dam that Ravan fell and became a laughing stock at a time when he was going around to the envy of all, showing off the boons he got from Brahma, and the Chandrahas he got from Shiv.

That river in which King Karthaveeryarjuna built the dam was none other than River Narmada, earlier known as Reva. This name can't be an unheard one at least to those Keralites who have some taste in literature and poetry. The reason is, in the famous poem 'Leela' by the celebrated poet Kumaran Asan, the mountainous area where Leela, the heroine of the poem was wandering in search of her lover Madanan, is on the shores of the River Reva. That story ends with Leela and Madanan committing suicide by jumping into the depths of River Reva. In Kalidasan's Mekhasandesam also, there is the mention of the River Reva.

This river occupies as significant a position as rivers Ganga, Yamuna or Sarayu in our epics. The hermitage of sage Jamadagni, father of Parasurama was on the bank of River Narmada. The famous Mahishmati Empire was also on the banks of Narmada. There are many references like this about this river in the epics and folklore.

There are many temples on the banks of River Narmada. Chowsath Yogini temple, Nemeswar Siddeswar Mandir, Chaubis Avatar temple, Maheswar temple, Omkareswar temple, Bhojpur Shiva temple, Bhimbetka temple etc are the prominent ones among them.

The banks of River Narmada have been the mute witnesses for many historic events. It was in a battle on the banks of River Narmada that King Pulikesan the 2nd of the Charaka dynasty of Karnataka, defeated king Harshawardhan of Kannauj. In a joint exploration conducted by the Archaeology Department of the Central Government and the Government of Madhya Pradesh, a lot of information has come out regarding the temples and archaeological sites on the banks of River Narmada. Fossils as old as 40 to 150 million years were found here. It is also discovered that, a part of River Narmada got submerged under the sea following an earthquake some 40 million years ago.

In all river beds, one can see boulders. These boulders acquire different sizes and shapes as they come tumbling down from the hillsides hitting against each other along with the flow of water. There is nothing unusual about it. But, in the case of the boulders in River Narmada, it is observed that most of those boulders are of the shape of Shivalingam. Believers call them 'Banalingam', and use them in the poojas. It is believed that the idol in the famous Brahadeeswara temple in Tanjavoor was picked from the Narmada River bed. That temple was built by Rajaraja Cholan.

At around 1300 km in length, River Narmada is the third longest river in India after Ganga and Godavari. However, she can claim to be the longest among the Indian rivers flowing towards the west. River Narmada is originating from some 1060 tiny springs in Amarkandak in the Vindhya-Satpura mountain ranges in Madhya Pradesh, and passes through Maharashtra and Gujarat, before ending up in the Gulf of Khambut to join the Arabian Sea. Thus, most of its course is through the laps of the Vindhya Mountains and the Western Ghats. The Vindhya-Satpura mountain ranges are considered the dividing line when we talk about the North and South Indias. River Narmada's main tributaries are Halan, Binjar, Hiren, Thava, Sekar, Kindhi, and Chota Thava from the south; and Butner, Shar, and Bunjar from the north. The Narmada River basin has the Vindhya Mountains on the north, Mykkala hill ranges on the east, Satpura mountain ranges on the south and the Arabian Sea on the west.

The Narmada River basin is 99000 sq. km in size spread over Madhya Pradesh, Gujarat, Maharashtra and Chhattisgarh; though the bulk (88%) of it is in Madhya Pradesh. Most of it is agricultural areas. Satpura Range, Aravalli Range, Sahyadri Range, Sabutara Range etc are the important hill ranges in the Narmada basin.

Whether Karthaveeryarjuna built a dam in River Narmada as mentioned in Ramayana or not, there are now several dams in this river. They include the famous Sardar Sarovar Dam, and also the smaller Indira Sagar Dam, Omkareswar Dam, Maheswar Dam, Bargi Dam, Maan Dam, Jobat Dam, Tava Dam etc. Of them, the Indira Dam constructed at Punasa in the Khandwa district in Madhya Pradesh can boast of having the largest reservoir in the country. This dam is 653 metres long and 92 metres high. It irrigates 650 sq. km of land and produces 1000 MW of power apart from providing 74,000,000 cu.m of water to various water supply schemes.

The development activities in River Narmada started way back in 1946 with the design of the Narmada Basin Irrigation Project. In it, there were four projects including the Sarovar dam. In 1950, the Central Water Power Commission decided to convert this into a hydroelectric project. River water dispute between Gujarat and Madhya Pradesh was in existence even then. To solve this, the Narmada River Water Dispute Authority was formed. In the year 1963, though the two State Governments discussed the issue, they could not reach an agreement. In 1965, the Khosla Committee report on the benefits of the Nawagam dam in River Narmada got published adding to the complexity of the issue.

In 1969 the Central Government formed the Narmada Water Dispute Tribunal to resolve the dispute between Gujarat and Madhya Pradesh. The Tribunal was formed with the Supreme Court judges Justice Ramaswamy, Justice Mathur and the retired judge V.P. Gopalan Nambiar as members. At this time, Rajasthan entered the fray raising certain claims over Narmada water.

In due course, the Tribunal announced its award. As per that, out of River Narmada's capacity of providing 28 million acre-feet (MAF) of water, Madhya Pradesh, Gujarat, Maharashtra and Rajasthan were to get 18.25 MAF, 9.0 MAF, 0.25 MAF and 0.50 MAF respectively. Further, the tribunal will monitor how each of these beneficiaries utilises their quota, and take corrective measures if found necessary. By now, the Government of Madhya Pradesh had taken proactive steps to take full advantage of the award. They had already planned 29 major projects, 135 medium projects and some 300 minor projects for River Narmada and its tributaries. Upper Narmada Project, Chinki Project, Dhooti Project, Sher Project etc are among them. It was also decided to have 520 km of canals with concrete lining, and allocate adequate funds for the rehabilitation of the affected people.

In 1980, the construction of the Sardar Sarovar Project started. But, soon the Ministry of Environment came out with an objection to it on grounds that appropriate environmental protection measures were not included in the project. With the environmental activists joining the fray, the matter became serious. They approached the World Bank which was financing the project. The opponents of the project led by Ms Medha Patkar formed the 'Narmada Bachao Andolan', and started an agitation demanding the scrapping of the project. Ms Patkar led the agitation supported by the people who were under the threat of eviction. This agitation had the backing of an organisation by the name National Alliance of People Movement (NAPM).

In 1981, the government appointed the Centre for Social Studies to find out how best the people of the 19 villages likely to be affected by the project could be resettled. By 1982, the voluntary organisations in Gujarat started getting involved in this. In 1983, the Central Government formed the National Water Resource Council (NWRC). The same year, the office of the Vice-President of the World Bank created the Social Policy and Resettlement Division with representation from all the parties involved. The Prime Minister, the Central Water Resource Minister and the State Chief Ministers were members of this council.

However, despite all the objections, the Central Government led by Mr. V.P. Singh stood firm and gave the 'go ahead' signal to the project. That triggered a series of agitations, and that attracted the attention of the media world over. The Sweden-based Right Livelihood Foundation honoured Ms Patkar with an award. She became so popular among the agitators that they started calling her fondly 'Medhaben'.

In September 1991, the Supreme Court intervened in this matter, and ordered to address all the contentious issues including the rehabilitation of the displaced. Later, in 1999, the Supreme Court granted permission for increasing the height of the dam to 85 metres. In 2002, the Indian Parliament approved the Inter-State Water Disputes Act. The Water Disputes Tribunals were given the same power as that of the Supreme Court. This helped speedy resolution of disputes. That very same year, the National Water Policy of India was revised to make it up-to-date, and in the year 2004, the height of the Sardar Sarovar Dam was further increased to 110 metres. The same year, the five generating stations of the dam became operational. Now, the Narmada water is used to irrigate 15 million acres of land. River Narmada also produces 3000 MW of power. Flowing mostly through Madhya Pradesh, she caters to the needs of Gujarat and Maharashtra also, to some extent.

These developments brought about big changes in the lives of the people in the region. Till some thirty years back, the travellers on the highways of Gujarat and Rajasthan used to get disturbed by the highly depressing sight of women trudging long distances with heavy water pots on their heads and hips. This was a common sight on the stretch of the road from Ahmedabad to Rajkot. I can vouch for this because it is in the States of Gujarat, Rajasthan, Maharashtra and Andhra Pradesh that I have moved around maximum, for conducting the environmental audits. But, such sights became old stories after increasing the height of the Sardar Sarovar dam which enabled water to reach far-flung areas through large canals.

That was not all. I remember that day when I and Mr. Raghu Srinivasan Iyengar, Director of the Houston-based ABS Industrial Verification Company were travelling from Ahmedabad to Rajkot around the time when the generating stations of the dam were being commissioned. On the way, we saw a mob ahead stopping vehicles. We were worried fearing that some disgruntled agitators were taking it out on the travellers. But, as we got nearer, we were in for a pleasant surprise because the mob was distributing sweets to the passers-by in celebration of the commissioning of the generators.

We can learn some lessons from the 'Narmada Bachao Andolan'. The antagonism towards the dam was fuelled by the fear that thousands will become homeless as the dam submerges the villages. The agitators enjoyed the support of the World Commission of Dams also. Prominent personalities like Baba Amte, Aamir Khan, Arundhati Roy etc also threw their weight behind Ms Patkar. Still, finally, the government had its way, and the dam became a reality. However, the agitators could draw solace from the fact that the agitation succeeded in the displaced persons getting compensated adequately. One can say, this was a win-win situation for both sides. It is the resolve, the conviction of the government which pulled it off. The fact that the agitations were by and large peaceful also helped.

While talking about the 'Narmada Bachao Andolan' of Ms Medha Patkar, the 'Chipko Andolan', a non-violent, satyagraha-based forest conservation movement comes to my mind. The Hindi word *chipko* means "to hug"; and reflects the tactic of embracing the trees to thwart the wood cutters. The first Chipko protest occurred near the Mandal village in the upper Alaknanda valley in April 1973. The villagers, having been denied access to a small number of trees to build agricultural tools, were outraged when the government allotted a much larger number to a sports goods manufacturer. When their appeals were denied, social activist Mr. Chandi Prasad Bhatt, founder of Dasholi Gram Swarajya Mandal [DGSM]), an organization to foster small industries for rural villagers using local resources, led the villagers into the forest, and embraced the trees to prevent cutting. It worked, and the government canceled the company's logging permit, and allotted the trees to the villagers.

With this success in Mandal, the DGSM workers and Mr. Sunderlal Bahuguna, a local environmentalist, began to deploy Chipko's tactics throughout the region. One of the next major protests occurred in 1974 near the village of Reni where more than 2,000 trees were scheduled to be felled. However, demonstrators led by one Ms. Gaura Devi forced the loggers to withdraw. The 'Chipko Andolan' went on to become the front-runner of many environment-related movements, and Mr. Sunderlal Bahuguna became a national level environmental activist.

Narmada river basin is not the only beneficiary of River Narmada's blessings. Through the Kshipra link project, River Narmada has come to the rescue of a river by name Kshipra flowing through the city of Ujjain of Poet Kalidasan fame, which had gone almost dry for many years. The Kshipra link project constructed at a cost of 432 crores of rupees, pumps River Narmada's water to a height of 1000 feet through 6 giant size pipes to a specially constructed tank in the Kshipra River. This water flows through the river for 115 km to reach Ujjain to solve the water problems of some 3000 villages and 70 small towns in the Malwa region. The success of this project has paved the way for more such schemes in the other rivers also.

River Narmada is one of the five holy rivers in India. Each one of them has its exclusive rituals and functions. River Narmada also has a ritual known as 'Narmada Parikrama'. Narmada Parikrama is the pilgrimage in which the devotees go to the origin of the river at the Maikkal Hills in Amarkhand in Madhya Pradesh, and walk barefoot from there all the way till Bharuch where the river joins the sea, and from there walk back to where they started. Thus, it is a long walk totalling 2600 km, taking months. During the walk, they also visit the temples on the way. One can imagine the degree of faith of a person who walks barefoot day and night over this much distance. They stay in the hermitages and auberges or inns or alms-houses along the way. For those who can't walk, the tour operators have arranged boat rides or tourist buses through parallel courses. Devotees address the river 'Narmada Maiyya' meaning Narmada, the mother.

When it comes to pollution, it has to be admitted that River Narmada too is not spared from it, confirming that in any situation, the rivers are the ultimate sufferers of reckless industrialisation as well as projects in the name of development without appropriate planning. It is a big paradox that the same people who consider rivers holy and call them 'mother', have no hesitation to subject the rivers to any atrocities or sacrilegious activities.

Coming to cruelties on mothers, that won't come as a surprise for River Narmada. As per legend, it is on her shores that Parasuraman alias Bhargavaraman beheaded his mother Renuka on the orders of his father Jamadagni. That story is, the ashram of hermit Jamadagni was on the bank of Narmada. One evening, Renuka went to the river to fetch water essential for her husband to conduct his evening pooja. But, Renuka had to wait because, at that time, the king of Haihayas, King Karthaveeryarjuna was bathing in the river along with his many wives in an exuberant mood. Once they left, Renuka went down to the river only to find that the water had become turbid due to the bathers' bustles. So she went upstream; but, there she found the Gandharva King Chitraradhan and his wives bathing. So, Renuka had to wait there also.

Finally, when she could collect the water and return to the ashram, it was night, well beyond the evening prayer time of hermit Jamadagni. An incensed Jamadagni called his sons and told them to kill their mother. As the elder sons declined the order one by one, the hermit finally came to the youngest among them, Parasuraman. The dutiful son did as his father ordered. But, this story had a happy ending because, when the hermit asked the obedient son what reward he wanted for being so faithful to his father, the son promptly requested to bring his mother back to life.

If the fate of mother earth is anything to go by, the history of children killing their mother is repeating itself. These are the days of people who have no hesitation to destroy our hills and rivers and forests and farmlands chasing easy money.

Rivers are our eternal mothers. They are more important to us than even our biological mothers because while the biological mothers gave us birth and saw us through our early years, the rivers sustain not only us throughout our entire lives; but also our future generations for all the time to come. So, let us resolve to do everything possible to protect them.

# YAMUNA

## Childhood Play-mate of Lord Krishna

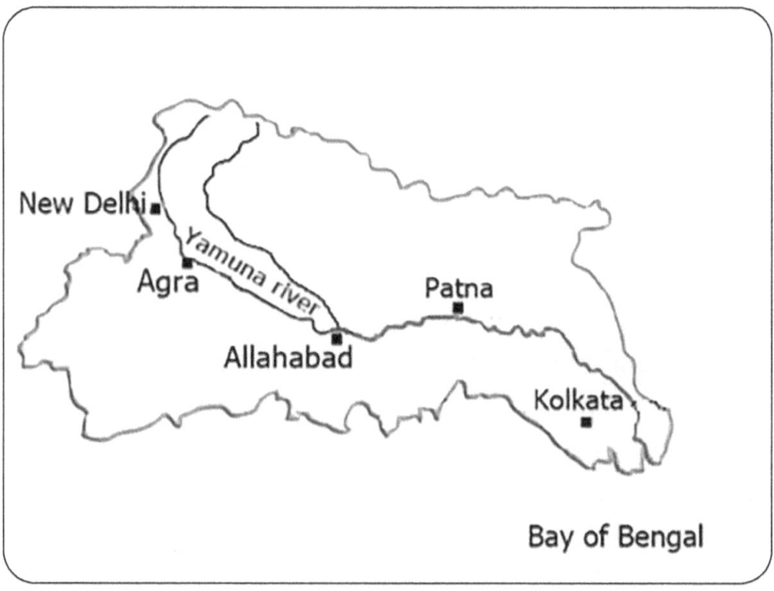


**Yamuna River**

In this whole world, nowhere other than in India, one can see a river and its banks providing the perfect backdrop for the literary work of all kinds, through hundreds of generations spanning thousands of years. In this country, there is hardly any luminary in the literary field who hasn't written poems or stories about a garden on the bank of that river, and about a boy who grew up frolicking in those surroundings. It is the magic of this river that, the more one writes about it, the more the urge to write more. The name of that river is Yamuna, the garden on its bank is the

Brindavan Gardens, and that boy is none other than Lord Krishna of the epic Mahabharata.

There is no other river like River Yamuna which has inspired creative minds across all languages and cultures to scale unprecedented heights in their vocations. Who won't be energised to try new vistas stimulated by the mesmerising beauty of the Brindavan gardens on the banks of River Narmada, and the allure in the sensual union of Lord Krishna with his sweetheart Radha in that garden in the romantic ambience created by the music of his flute and the babble of this river?

In the epic Mahabharatha, River Yamuna is called Kalindi. As per that, this river originates from the Kalinda mountains, flows through Indraprasth, and joins River Ganga. Madhura, where Lord Krishna was born, was on the banks of River Yamuna. It is written in Bhagavatham that, in the night when Lord Krishna was born, as his father Vasudev took him and fled to save the baby from Kamsa who had sworn to kill him, River Yamuna parted to make way for him to cross over. Who can forget the scene of Krishna dancing on the hood of Kaliyan, the five-headed demon snake which poisoned the River Kalindi? Devotees worship the Yamuna on par with River Ganga. According to mythology, Yamuna is the sister of Yeman, and Ganga is the daughter of the Sun.

As River Kalindi flows down from the epics to modern history, she acquires the name Yamuna, and continues her journey enduring the pain of invasions and subjugations by alien regimes, and the abuse at the hands of everyone who ironically depends on her directly or indirectly for their survival. Though technically the status of River Yamuna is as a tributary of River Ganga, with a length of 1376 km, she is bigger than many full-fledged rivers.

The origin of the River Yamuna is at the snow-clad Yamunotri in the State of Uttarakhand in the lap of the Himalayas mountain ranges. To be more exact, the starting point is Saptharshi Kundam above Yamunotri which is 90 km away from Rishikesh at an elevation of 3200 metres above MSL. Devotees believe that taking bath in the hot water springs here has medicinal as well as spiritual benefits. After this, the river reaches Yamuna Nagar in Haryana. There is a dam by the name Tajewala here. From this dam, water flows to two canals on the east and west sides. The canal on the western side goes to Karnal, Panipat etc to meet the water needs of those areas. The canal towards the east takes water to Haryana and Uttar Pradesh, including the Wasirabad Barrage near Delhi.

There are so many canals like this in River Yamuna. The Agra canal built in 1874 starts from the Okla barrage and reaches River Banganga. There is also another canal by the name Munak made way back in 1819. This canal, starting from Karnal, and reaching Delhi was refurbished in 2008. Right now, the construction of the Sutlej – Yamuna link canal, popularly known as SYL Canal which is for taking Yamuna water to Punjab is progressing. This canal, once completed, will enable sharing of water in rivers Ravi and Beas between Haryana and Punjab. Delhi – Faridabad, and Delhi – Agra are the major waterways in River Yamuna.

River Yamuna reaches Uttar Pradesh next. It is at Allahabad that the Yamuna joins with Ganga. The mythical River Saraswati is supposed to join Yamuna and Ganga here making it the Triveni Sangamam. There is another dam awaiting Yamuna as she reaches the Doon Valley covering some 200 km from her origin at Yamunotri. From here, Yamuna flows south to Pavntha Sahib. There is an important Sikh temple here. It was built by Guru Gobind Singh, the founder and supreme leader of the Sikh community.

River Yamuna has her tributaries, the longest among them being the 960 km long Chambal River. This river starts from Manpur. It is at Itawa where Chambal meets the Yamuna that, the Gandhi Sagar dam is located. Jawahar Nagar dam, Pratap dam, Kota barrage etc are also in River Chambal.

The Sutlej – the Yamuna link canal project has a lot of peculiarities. Out of its 210 km length, 120 km is in Punjab and 90 km is in Haryana. As per the memorandum of understanding signed between these two States, 4.46 lakh hectares of land in Haryana, and 1.28 lakhs hectares of land in Punjab could be irrigated by this project. The part of the canal on the Haryana side was completed time bound in 1990. However, with the murder of the Chief Engineer and the Superintending Engineer of the project in the Punjab side on July 23, 1990, activities there came to a standstill. The attitude of the government of Punjab towards this project was lukewarm from the very start, and it became worse after those murders. So, the government of Haryana approached the Supreme Court with a request to restart the work, and the court ordered Punjab to honour its commitment to the project. But, the government of Punjab didn't comply with it. Instead, they approached the court with a plea against the project. However, the Supreme Court rejected it and ordered the Central Public Works Department to complete the project. But, nothing much has happened even after that.

The National Water Development Agency is an agency working under the Central Government. It is the Upper Yamuna Board which is authorised to handle the projects. The representatives of Himachal Pradesh, Haryana, Uttar Pradesh, and Rajasthan are the members of this Board. Kishavo, Renuka, Lakhwar Byasi etc are the dams planned in this project. Rajasthan is using the Yamuna water to irrigate two districts. Apart from this, the Panjeswar dam is planned in the Mahakali River. This dam is 315 metres tall. It is made with clay and granite. Once completed, this will be the tallest dam in the world to have been made with this material. Its reservoir will have a capacity of 11.35 billion cum, and it will be spread over 11600 hectares of land. This will be the largest reservoir in the Himalayan region. 5040 MW of electricity also will be produced from here. Thus, this will be one of the largest hydroelectric projects in India.

Many of the tourist attractions in the country are on the banks of Yamuna. Places like Madhura, Delhi, Agra etc were the venues of many events of historic importance also. Madhura on its banks draws its fame as the city of Kamsa, the husband of the daughters of Jera Sandhan whose fame came from imprisoning 87 kings. River Yamuna saw Bhim who defeated that same Jerasandhan in wrestling, and also witnessed Yudhishtir ascending to the golden throne. River Yamuna also had the good fortune to quench the thirsts of Yudhishtir and his brothers as they were wandering in a forest after losing everything in the game of dices to the Kauravas.

Right from the Mauryas to the Mughals who were displaced by the British colonialists, River Yamuna has been witness to so many wars as well as the rise and fall of so many empires like those of Emperor Ashoka, Chandragupta, Harsha and Kanishka to Aurangzeb and Bahadur Sha. River Yamuna also had the misfortune to be the mute witness to the sufferings of the Indian people under the misrule of the puppets whom the earliest invaders Muhammad Ghouri and Muhammad Ghazni foisted as the rulers on them, as the kings returned to their countries. River Yamuna also saw the ascension to power of the dynasties of Khilji, Tughlaq and Lodhi; and later Babar defeating Ibrahim Lodhi, the last of the Lodhis, for him and his successors to rule the country for the next two centuries. However, all of them were consigned to the history books and their descendants disappeared without a trace.

River Yamuna also witnessed the rule of Humayun, Akbar, Jahangir, Sha Jahan and of course Aurangazeb who killed his brothers and imprisoned his father Sha Jahan to ascend to the throne. During the 8 years till his death on January 22, 1666 Emperor Sha Jahan spent in the Agra Fort as a prisoner with his eyes keyed on to the Taj Mahal at a distance, he had only the breeze from River Yamuna to assuage his hurt feelings.

In the battle of Plazi in 1757, the British captured Bengal to get a toehold in India, and gradually established their hegemony over the southern and northern areas of the country. Then, as River Yamuna watched helplessly, the British captured Delhi, easily displacing the shaky descendants of Aurangaseeb. With that, their enslavement of India for the next two centuries started. But, River Yamuna could draw solace from the fact that she could also watch the resurgence of the spirit of nationalism in India culminating in bringing the British down to their knees. One can hardly find another river which has witnessed as many momentous historical events as River Yamuna.

Talking about the cities on the banks of River Yamuna, of course, Delhi comes first. It is the historical city of Indraprastam which later on became Delhi. Initially, Calcutta was the capital of British India. It was in 1911 that they shifted the capital to Delhi. It was an Architect by the name of Mr. Edwin Lutein who designed New Delhi. It is said that from 1912, it took 20 years of untiring effort to complete this job. This design accommodated the Mughal and Buddhist heritages of Delhi.

After Delhi, the next big city on the bank of the Yamuna is Agra. It was a Sultan named Sikandar Lodhi who built Agra. After the death of this Sultan, his son Ibrahim Lodhi took charge. As Babar defeated Ibrahim Lodhi in the battle of Panipat in the year 1526, and established the Mughal rule, Agra became the nerve centre of the Mughal Empire. Etawah, Allahabad etc are the other important cities on the banks of River Yamuna.

Now, the bad news. For a long, River Yamuna is notorious as the most polluted river in the world. Some 70% of all those polluting matter are entering the Yamuna waters during her flow in a 45 km section near Delhi which is less than 4% of the total length of the river. It is the community discharges which cause most of the damage. Paradoxically, the materials used in many religious functions which are later discarded in the river also play a none too insignificant part in fouling up the Yamuna waters. The accusation that Yamuna is the most polluted river in the world is not mere hearsay; but, supported by technical data on water taken from different places which are as follows.

The presence of faecal coliform bacteria at Nizamabad, Kalindikunj, Okla and Badalpur was found to be 540000, 170000, 270000 and 240000 respectively. The same is the picture when it comes to total coliform. The pH value of water at a place called Palla was found to be 8.9 which is too alkaline for domestic use. In short, forget drinking, Yamuna water is unfit even for bathing or farming in the stretch around Delhi.

As per the government's own admission, the discharges from 18 drainage systems are reaching River Yamuna once she leaves the Vazirabad barrage. More than 100 tonnes of solid waste also reach the river here every day. This is far more than the capacity of a river to clean itself. It is into this river that industrial wastes also are reaching. With that, Yamuna turns more poisonous than even that old Kalindi poisoned by the snake

Kaliyan. One shouldn't forget that this is happening to the river flowing at a stone's throw away from the Indian Parliament building, the seat of the Government of India; and even more bizarrely, that river is meeting 70% of the water requirement of Delhi including that of the Parliamentarians.

On this, I would like to draw a parallel to a case related to River Thames flowing close to the British parliament. Once, it so happened that people noticed a lot of froth in the river, and the investigations revealed that the reason behind it was some kind of pollution. The members of Parliament rose in unison against this, and the problem was solved on a war footing. Similarly, in New Zealand, the government there raised the status of River Vansui to that of an individual. This was aimed at protecting the river banks and facilitating the free flow of the river.

But, unfortunately for River Yamuna, Indian parliament members are more concerned about their gains in whatever they do, rather than in the matters of public interest. However, Mr. Muhammad Salim, a human rights activist initiated legal action to give River Yamuna, a status as an individual similar to that of River Vansui. In 2017, the High Court of Uttarakhand granted it. As per that, River Yamuna is entitled to all the rights a citizen enjoys; hence, disfiguring or causing any harm to River Yamuna is a cognizable offence. How this translates into action is a matter of conjectures.

It is not that the government is passive to the problems in River Yamuna. In 1993, the government initiated the massive 'Yamuna Action Plan' with the cooperation of the Japanese Government modelled in line with the 'Ganga Action Plan'. This plan envisages freeing Delhi and its satellite town and nearby cities like Muzafir Nagar, Ghaziabad, Noida, Brindaban, Madhura, Agra, Itawa, Yamuna Nagar, Karnal, Panipat, Sonipat, Gurugram, Faridabad in the region of all the polluting discharges, and thereby saving River Yamuna of this scourge.

As per this plan, this project which kick-started in 1993, was to be completed by the year 2000. Of course, as usual, it slipped behind schedule, and had to be extended for another 3 years. During this time, they built drains in the cities to divert the community discharges into the processing plants before discarding them into the river. Effluent treatment plants were made mandatory for industrial units as well. However, it is said that due to the lack of support from the general public, the 'Yamuna Action Plan' couldn't produce the expected results. One of the reasons for it is rumoured to be the failure of the authorities in making it a people's movement by educating and mobilising people against pollution, and thus ensuring public participation which is essential for the success of any community-based reform.

If matters don't improve, perhaps it may require a reincarnation of Lord Sri Krishna to save River Yamuna. In his last birth, as a punishment for the crime of polluting River Kalindi alias Yamuna, Krishna trashed and subdued the snake Kaliyan, and even danced on his hood before castigating him to the uninhibited Ramanaka Island. The young Krishna did so agitated over the fate of the humans, animals and birds who quenched their thirst in the poisoned Kalindi.

Hopefully, Krishna will visit again to save his favourite river from the mindless exploitation and ill-treatment at the hands of modern-day Kaliyans. Or, at least send someone with the unshakeable resolve to save River Yamuna from such elements.

# VAIGAI

## Memories of Sangh Period

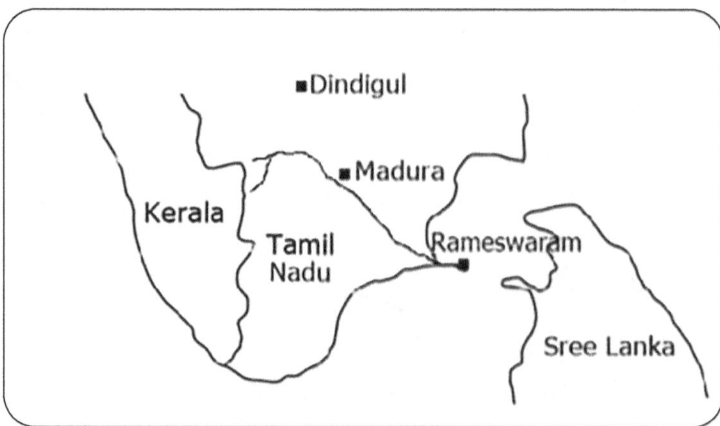



**Vaigai River**

There is a Tamil poem which spread the fame of Tamil Nadu far and wide with its class. That poem's title is 'Chilappathikaram'. That is the story of the tears and fortitude of a destitute woman by the name of Kannaki, penned by the respected poet Ilango Adigal. It starts from an obscure village on the banks of River Kaveri, and ends at the city of Madurai on the banks of River Vaigai. River Vaigai flows like the life of Kannaki, the heroine of Chilappathikaram, reliving the memories of the huge tragedy, Kannaki's life was.

The origin of River Vaigai, as per the epics, is like this. As Lord Shiva came to Madurai for his marriage with Meenakshi, in Shiva's entourage, there was a man by name Kumbhodaran who was rather infamous for his insatiable hunger and thirst. As a thirsty Kumbhodaran started creating ruckus asking for water, Lord Shiva uttered the words 'Vai Kai' - meaning 'place your hand' – and released River Ganga from his tufted lock of hair. The water which fell into the outstretched hand (kai) of Kumbhodaran spilt over and flowed down to get christened as Vai-Kai or Vaigai. Since the river was a gift from Shiva, she is also known as Shiva Ganga.

I saw River Vaigai for the first time during my visit to Madurai for the treatment of my eyes which were inflicted with macular degeneration. My eyesight then had reached its nadir. My visit to Madurai was for a final attempt to save my eyes at the Arvind Hospital there, after the doctors treating me back home raised their hands. The season was the peak of summer.

As an environmental engineer, my job involved a lot of travel, and I had the habit of using those trips also to visit the places of interest in and around my destination. I didn't deviate from it in this trip also, even though it was for an unpleasant medical purpose. In fact, during the planning stages of this travel to Madurai itself, I had in mind visits to the Madurai Meenakshi Temple, River Vaigai etc.

So, as I started from Madurai airport to my hotel, I sounded the driver of the taxi to alert me if River Vaigai is on the way. He nodded. Then, after covering some distance, he stopped the car and told me "Sir, over there is River Vaigai". I had the shock of my life as I looked out. What I saw through my almost lifeless eyes was only a stretch of farmland growing various kinds of vegetables. Is this the divine river supposed to be quenching the thirst of the city of Madurai, and extolled as a glamorous Tamil beauty in many songs? Here, right in front of my eyes, it is all vegetable gardens with only a few tiny water channels here and there. I could also see some excavators and trucks on the dry river bed.

As I learnt more about River Vagai, I realised that River Vaigai is dry for more than 6 months a year. There is a saying among the villagers that Vaigai will come to life only when it rains in the adjacent State of Kerala. That is more or less true because River Vaigai gets water released from the dams in rain-rich Kerala. Kerala dams open during the rainy season as they get filled up beyond capacity. But, occasionally, during times when River Vaigai goes completely dry also, the Kerala authorities use to release water into Vaigai.

River Vaigai is originating from the Varasanat Hills near Theni in the Periyar Plateau in the Western Ghats. From there, she flows in a north-east direction through the Kamban Valley which is lying between the Palani Hills on the north and Varasunad Hills on the south; and then turns in the south-east direction. Then she goes east and heads towards Tamil Nadu. The famous Vattappara waterfalls are in River Vaigai. Crossing the Vattappara waterfalls, River Vaigai reaches Madurai on her way to join Palk Strait, its destination in the Ramanathapuram district. It is another misfortune of this river that, it was not destined to join a sea directly like most other rivers.

*(Palk Strait is a strait or channel between the State of Tamil Nadu in India and the Jaffna district of Sri Lanka. It connects the Bay of Bengal in the north-east and the Palk Bay in the south-west. It is 40 to 85 miles wide and 85 miles long. It is here that River Vaigai ends. There is a chain of natural limestone shoals between Pamban Island off Tamil Nadu and Mannar Island off Sri Lanka in this, collectively known as Adam's Bridge, and also Rama Sethu.)*

At Theni, River Kiruthamal joins Vaigai. The name Kiruthamal is mentioned in the epic Mahabharatha. In the 'Matsyavathara' story, it was while performing the rites in the Kiruthamal river that Manu got the 'talking fish', the first incarnation of Mahavishnu. It is this fish which reclaimed the Vedas from Hayagreevan and saved Manu and the seven sages from the grand floods. Churuliyar, Manjalar, Varattar, Tagalar etc also are the tributaries of River Vaigai.

Kambam, Theni, Dindigul, Madurai, Sivaganga, Ramanadhapuram etc are the towns on the banks of the 258 km long River Vaigai. Madurai was the capital of the Pandya Dynasty of the yesteryears. The world-famous Meenakshi Temple is situated in Madurai. Historians believe that this temple was built between AD 1623 and 1655 by King Kulasekhara of the Pandya Dynasty. There are 14 towers in this temple. The 170 feet tall southern tower is the tallest among them. It is calculated that there are some 33000 sculptures in this temple. The 1000 pillar Mandapam (structure) which in reality has only 988 pillars is world famous for its architectural marvel.

Among the other attractions in and around Madurai are the Teppakkulam, Ecopark, Tiruppuram Kundram, Alagar Koil etc.

Theppakkulam is a huge pond with roads on all four sides, and a small temple on an island at its centre.

Ecopark is a garden with colour lights, in the middle of the city.

Tiruppuram Kundram is a beautiful cave temple some 10 km from Madurai. It is believed that the marriage of Indran's daughter Devasena with Subrahmanyan took place here. In this temple, there are the idols of Siva, Vishnu, Durga, Ganapathy, Vedavyasan etc.

Alagar Koil is a temple some 19 km away from Madurai. This temple also is famous for its architectural beauty.

There is only one dam in this river. That is the Vaigai Dam in the Theni district. Vaigai Dam was built in the year 1898 by the British for drinking water distribution. The reservoir of this dam was connected to the Mullapperiyar dam in Kerala. These days, up to 85% of water in the Vaigai dam is coming from the Mullapperiyar dam. It is said that the Pandya kings were very particular about making maximum use of Vaigai water. It is also said that there were 153 communities on the banks of Vaigai. Near the end of the 18th century, there was a big drought; and that was the reason for the construction of the dams at Mullapperiyar and Vaigai. Once upon a time, River Vaigai was the venue for the colourful Chithirai Thiruvizha festival.

'Chithira Thiruvizha', also known as Meenakshi Thirukalyanam is a famous, month-long festival of Tamil Nadu. It takes place in the Tamil month of 'Chithirai' which coincides with the mid-April to mid-May days. According to the folklore, the Pandya King Malayadwajan and his wife

Kanjanamala were issueless. Thinking that this was due to the anger of Gods, they started to conduct poojas and other religious rituals. During the progression of one such ritual, from nowhere, a beautiful young girl appeared and sat on the king's lap. Simultaneously, everyone there heard an oracle from the space announcing that this girl is the incarnation of Shakthi, the wife of Lord Shiva; and one day, Shiva himself will come here to take her.

The royal couple named the girl Meenakshi, and she grew up in the palace as the princess. In due course, she learnt martial arts and ascended to the throne after the death of the king. Queen Meenakshi went on a conquering spree and annexed all the neighbouring kingdoms to Madurai. After that, she went to the Himalayas to conquer Shiva's Kailasam and took on Lord Shiva. Impressed with the valour of Queen Meenakshi, Shiva fell in love with her. Cupid too played its part, and Meenakshi reciprocated the feeling. Lord Shiva told her "For now, you return to Madurai. I will come there and marry you." Meenakshi returned to Madurai.

In due course, Shiva reached Madurai and married Meenakshi. It is believed that it was on this occasion that River Vaigai was born to quench the thirst of Kumbhodaran as mentioned earlier.

Alagar festival is another important festival in Madurai. Even though this festival and the Meenakshi festival are separate entities, since the time of the Thirumala Naicker's rule in Madurai, they are celebrated contiguously.

There is a story behind this also. As per that, Alagar was the brother of Meenakshi. (It appears, King Malayadwajan got this son after adopting Meenakshi). Unfortunately, Alagar could reach for the marriage of Meenakshi only late. So, unable to face Meenakshi, Alagar left leaving on a platform on the other side of Vaigai all the gifts he had brought for her. That is why the Alagar festival is celebrated after the Meenakshi festival, but in continuation, says the story.

During the past 3 years, I have visited Madurai at least 20 times in connection with the treatment of my eye, and every time I used to take strolls along the banks of River Vaigai. But, only once I was fortunate to see some water in Vaigai; which was, when the water was released from the Mullapperiyar dam. It was quite pleasing as well as touching to see the happiness of the people there at the sight of the water gushing down. What to say? People value things only when they don't have them. So, every time Kerala raises the Mullapperiyar issue in the Supreme Court demanding the decommissioning of the Mullapperiyar dam, River Vaigai will be sitting with her heart in her mouth as the judgment date approaches. Fortunately for her, till now, the Supreme Court hasn't conceded the pleas of Kerala.

Though minor in stature, when it comes to pollution, River Vaigai is in the major league. Sewerage apart, people living on the banks of this river often dump all kinds of waste materials in the river. Since this river is dry, or with measly flow for most of the year, those materials get accumulated to create huge problems. It requires a lot of effort to make the people aware of the environmental and social consequences of such uncivil practices, and desist from them.

It was on October 2nd, the Gandhi Jayanthi day in 2014 that the Vaigai restoration project was set rolling. People from all walks of life – teachers, students, social workers, the general public etc participated in that function. Public meetings and door-to-door publicity was given to make people aware of the consequences of polluting the river. On May 12, 2015, they organised a grand procession in which many renowned stage artists and film personalities participated. Some of the natives who had since settled abroad had flown back only for participating in the event. Madurai and its suburbs are famous cultural centres. Colourful tableaus depicting the heritage of Tamil Nadu, and other attractions like stills, cut-outs, band sets, dance, music etc added to the glamour of this procession. That was a grand show. The procession ended in a public meeting in which the crowd took the pledge to spare River Vaigai from the pollution of all kinds. But, if the situation in the river now is any indication, nothing much from that has translated into action; and the river is choking with dunes of waste materials.

Unless the State Government and the Madurai city corporation join hands and implement an integrated scheme as they did in the city of Ahmedabad on the banks of River Sabarmati, the dream of saving River Vaigai will remain unfulfilled. The Corporation of Madurai had installed a sewerage treatment plant there; but, being of insufficient capacity, it hasn't been able to do much in preventing the sewerage from finding its way into Vaigai. The incentives the authorities had declared were also insufficient. So also, the budget allocation for various schemes aimed at reducing the pollution in the river. For example, the amount spent on improvements in the river was a paltry Rs. 81.41 lakhs, and the budget for the sewerage treatment plant in Madurai city was only 2.5 crores.

In India, the second biggest Gandhi Museum after the original one at Sabarmati is at Madurai in the Rani Mangammal Palace donated by the Tamil Nadu government. It was opened to the public on April 15, 1959 by the then Prime Minister of India, Pandit Jawaharlal Nehru. I had the good fortune to visit both Sabarmati and Madurai museums. Except for the sentimental importance of the Sabarmati ashram as the original one where Gandhi lived, material-wise the Madurai Museum is not inferior to the one at Sabarmati in any big way.

Unless there are the concerted efforts of all the agencies involved, and provide adequate resources, nothing much will be achieved in improving the condition of River vaigai. When the Gujarat government is spending 1200 crores of rupees to beautify River Sabarmati, can't the Tamil Nadu government spend at least a fraction of it on River Vaigai? Not only that; in Ahmedabad, they have created a volunteer force of 20,000 people for protecting River Sabarmati. There are no such schemes to save poor River Vaigai. The government should make a master plan involving the general public in a big way giving them the ownership of the project and allocating sufficient funds to make River Vaigai also as beautiful as River Sabarmati.

The Kavari – Vaigai – Gundar project will become a reality pretty soon. Though this project doesn't give much importance to the beautification of River Vaigai, that will give a shot in the arm to the agriculture sector of the Pudukkottai-Shivaganga-Ramanathapuram districts. The estimated cost of this 262 km-long link project is 14,400 crores. Some 2300 acres of land will come under its irrigation. This project will have a 150 km long canal from Vellar to Vaigai. Another canal of 34 km will run from Vaigai to Gundar. This project will facilitate utilising the flood waters presently going to waste, and raise the water table. That will recharge some 342 lakes and ponds to fulfil that long cherished ambition of Tamil Nadu. At one time, there were so many lakes and wells and ponds in River Vaigai; but hardly any now. The food production of Tamil Nadu is expected to increase by 20% once this project is completed.

As I said at the beginning, it was with my parched, almost lifeless eyes that I saw River Vaigai for the first time in her equally or even more pathetic condition. Thanks to the expert care of the doctors like Ms Indu Kumar at the Aravind Hospital in Madurai, my eyes got rejuvenated to some extent. But, unfortunately for River Vaigai, her lot remains more or less the same, and her rejuvenation seems quite some distance away.

River Vaigai may not have a prominent place among the rivers in India. But, one shouldn't forget that no other river in India can claim the rich cultural pedigree of River Vaigai as the river which has in her lap the city of Madurai considered the cradle of the great Dravidian Culture.

As per the folklore, as the rain clouds gather in the skies, the peacocks will start dancing, and the hornbills - who, the villagers believe, can't drink with their necks bent down, and hence have to wait till the rains so that the rain drops from above can fall into their raised beaks - will stay focussed looking up at the skies with their mouths wide open. If that is true, every time the lightning and thunder forewarn the opening of the skies, River Vaigai and the hornbills by her side, should be looking up eagerly at the skies with prayers on their lips.

I too join that prayer. How I wish to see River Vaigai flowing majestically in all the seasons as her sisters elsewhere!

# RHINE
## Echoes of Epic Battle

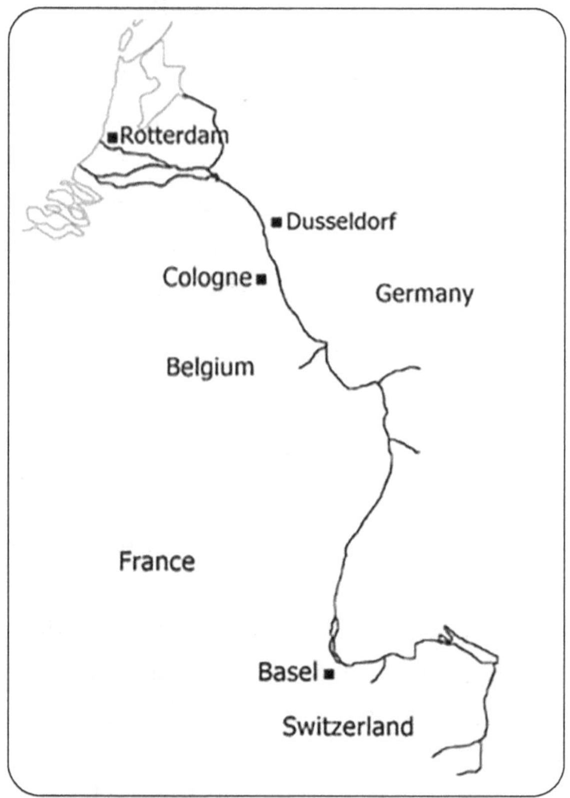


**Rhine River**

There is only one river in the whole world which had the misfortune of witnessing from close range the miseries of mankind from both the world wars. That river is also the longest river in Germany, the country which ascended to the position of a world power gaining from the weakening of France post Napoleon. 'Rhine' is the name of that river. River Rhine also watched the eclipse of mighty Germany after the First World War; as well as its recovery later under Adolf Hitler, only to collapse again by the end of the Second World War. This river also saw Germany becoming the financial powerhouse of Europe in the later years.

Ever since I learned about River Rhine in the school curriculum, I dreamt of not only seeing that river; but also, even enjoying a boat ride in it. 'Dreamt' because, in those days, for a schoolboy from the remote Kattoor village in Kerala, a trip to even the nearest town Trichur was too rare an event. However, by the time I grew up, the world had changed a lot making international travel a routine affair for most professionals. I too joined that trend for destiny to take me to Germany.

That break came to me on a platter when I was selected as one of the three delegates to participate in a conference held at Dusseldorf in the 1980s during my stint as the Head of the Department of Environment and Safety with the Government of Dubai. Mr. Salim Mesmar, Director of the Department of Health, and Mr. Hamdhan Al Shar from the Environment Division were the other members in our team.

Dusseldorf is less than 300 km from the Frankfurt International Airport. The other members of the delegation agreed to my suggestion that instead of taking a flight, we go by a cruise ship from Frankfurt to Dusseldorf along the River Rhine. That paved the way for the fulfilment of my long cherished dream.

River Rhine's origin is from the Vorderhein and the Hinterrhein springs located at 2300 metres above MSL in the Alps Mountain Ranges in Switzerland. Flowing through the Litcherstine valleys in Switzerland in the early part of its journey, the river passes through the mountain gorges between Switzerland and Austria, and soon gathers speed and volume on its way to Lake Constance, a source of drinking water for large parts of southern Germany. After this, River Aare, Rhine's main tributary joins Rhine, and a while later, River El from France and River Neko from Germany also join River Rhine. Going further, River Rhine flows through the industrial town of Basel in Switzerland, and over the famous Rhine Falls at Schaffhausen.

As River Rhine enters Germany, it becomes the border between Germany and France. Moving on, as it enters the Rhine Gorge, the landscape changes again. Here, with a valley filled with vineyards and castles overlooking her, the river narrows down. Finally, River Rhine reaches the Netherlands, a completely flat country. There several other rivers joins her as she flows into the North Sea at Rotterdam. Occasionally, during the months of February – March when the River Rhine gets flooded with the water from the snow melted in the Alps, the river may take detours in its course in its delta region.

Rotterdam, where the Rhine joins the sea, is an ancient port city. In the olden days, River Rhine was the main channel for the transportation of goods arriving at the port to the interiors. In the Second World War, many of the old constructions there were destroyed. Later on, though the Dutch attempted some restoration jobs like what the Germans did in Berlin, they were not as successful.

The 1,232 km long Rhine flows through six countries - Switzerland, Principality of Liechtenstein, Austria, Germany, France and The Netherlands. River Rhine is known by different names as it flows from country to country. For example, she is Rhein in Germany; Rhine in France and Rijn in the Netherlands, similar to our River Brahmaputra taking the name Jamuna as she enters Bangladesh. Once upon a time, it was River Rhine and River Danube that was considered the boundaries of the Roman Empire. In Europe, River Rhine is the second most important river after River Danube. This river is Western Europe's most important waterway. Navigable from Basel to Rotterdam, it serves as a highway for Europe's freight movement.

The scenery I could enjoy during my cruise from Frankfurt to Dusseldorf is beyond description in words. First and foremost, no depressing and nauseating uncivil activities anywhere along the river banks. No unsightly encroachments jutting out into the river or haphazard constructions. At some places, one can see the remnants of old forts and garrisons which were there to defend against the invaders coming from across the river. The mounds and hills on the banks of the river are providing such an arresting view in the background of the mountains far away. Trees, Plants and birds alien to us are also seen along the banks.

The houses, resorts and the other buildings on the mountain slopes stand as testimony to the affluence and the advancement in the architectural capabilities of modern Germany. This cruise reminded me of a similar experience in the Thousands Island Lake in Canada. It is said that, most of those islands are owned by Hollywood celebrities, the same way as the mansions on the hillsides along River Rhine are owned by European multi-millionaires. Near Dusseldorf is the city of Cologne, where there is a dome of historical importance attracting tourists. Near this dome, I found a conman trying to cheat the unsuspecting tourists with fake jewellery.

## River Pollution

The main purpose of having this chapter on the River Rhine is to give an idea to the esteemed readers about the way the Europeans handle the pollution problems in their rivers in stark contrast to what the authorities in our country do. Here is a brief on the history of the pollution on the River Rhine; and how that was dealt with.

Warning bells on the bad state of River Rhine were first rang way back in the 19th century itself when local fishermen found that some breeds of fish were vanishing in the river. But, nobody knew what to do in those days when there were no systems in existence for the treatment of sewerage and other waste. Later, by the end of the Second World War, with more and more industries coming up, the Salmons too disappeared, and many communities living around River Rhine became convinced that all was not well with the river.

Thus, for decades, untreated wastes of all kinds were flowing into River Rhine, and it reached a peak in the late 1940s. The proliferation of heavy industries along the river-banks, hydro-electric projects, freight boats, excess traffic etc destroyed much of the river's ecosystem. Nowhere was the damage more serious than in the Swiss city of Basel which is famous for its chemical and pharmaceutical industries. While these businesses brought prosperity to Basel, they also discharged dangerous waste materials into the river. Compounding the problem, Basel had no sewerage treatment plant in those days. So even the municipal wastes flowed directly into the river. As a result of all these, fish and plant life started to disappear, and swimmers in the Rhine developed skin rashes.

Once matters reached this stage, it didn't take too long for the governments to act. In 1950, they formed the International Commission based at Basel for the Protection of Rhine. Representatives of Switzerland, Germany and France worked together from Basel to keep the river clean. In 1963, the countries through which the Rhine flows signed the Rhine Action Programme (RAP) to protect the river. This plan which set ambitious goals for reducing pollution was time-bound to meet its objective by the year 2000.

This was followed by forming a lot of very strict international laws on what could be discharged into the River Rhine. Efforts were made to get the factories on the river's banks either to shift or to eliminate their harmful discharges. Needless to say, by now, private houses in and around Basel were connected to a sewerage treatment plant, thus stopping the flow of domestic waste directly into the river.

In the meantime, on November 1, 1986, a catalyst for improving River Rhine appeared in the form of a fire at a chemical plant at Basel's Schweizerhalle causing tonnes of toxic pesticides to leak into the river. Thousands of fish died, and some species, such as the eel, were wiped out. Within 10 days of the accident, the pollution travelled the length of the Rhine into the North Sea. This environmental catastrophe provided further impetus to the efforts to clean up the river. This accident served as a wake-up call for all those who had something or the other to do with the river.

Stringent actions followed. In Germany, for 24 hours a day, the monitoring station drew water from five different points along the river every six minutes, and checked it for dozens of different chemical elements. That made it difficult for the chemical industries to put anything into the river that should not be there. Polluters were traced and fined. As a result of all the anti-pollution measures taken by these countries jointly, the water in the river improved tremendously. The swimmers returned to the river; and so too the fish.

It was most heartening to know that, side by side with the laboratory tests to detect pollution, the authorities monitored the response of fish to the river water to reconfirm the efficacy of the anti-pollution drive. For this, every morning, Basel's cantonal fish inspector checked a fish cage near one of the river's dams. That cage had a specially designed 'fish ladder' to help the fish to cross the dam to proceed further in their migration route. Creating facilities for the fish to cross dams shows the commitment of the authorities in those countries toward the preservation of nature. But, that is not the point here. The fish inspector monitored the traffic of fish in the cage and found that the fish count was progressively increasing. The return of fish to the River Rhine was the best indication that the water quality was improving. Who else, other than fish can authoritatively certify the quality of water? What an idea!

The concerted efforts of six independent countries produced that result in a time-bound manner without any mutual accusations or 'passing the buck'. But, when it comes to matters related to our rivers, we find it near impossible to come to a consensus even between our own States. When the Europeans tackled the problem by forming the Rhine 'Action' Programme, it is the Water 'Dispute' Authorities that the circumstances here force us to create. That shows the true picture of the situation here.

Thinking of River Rhine, there is no doubt that this river has endured so much pain from witnessing so many natural calamities, disasters and bloodsheds like the great famine of the 14th century, the plague which followed it taking with it millions of lives; and of course, the world wars. I sincerely pray to God that River Rhine had enough; and hence, please spare her from more of such distresses in the rest of her life.

# ST. LAWRENCE
## Foot Prints of Invasions

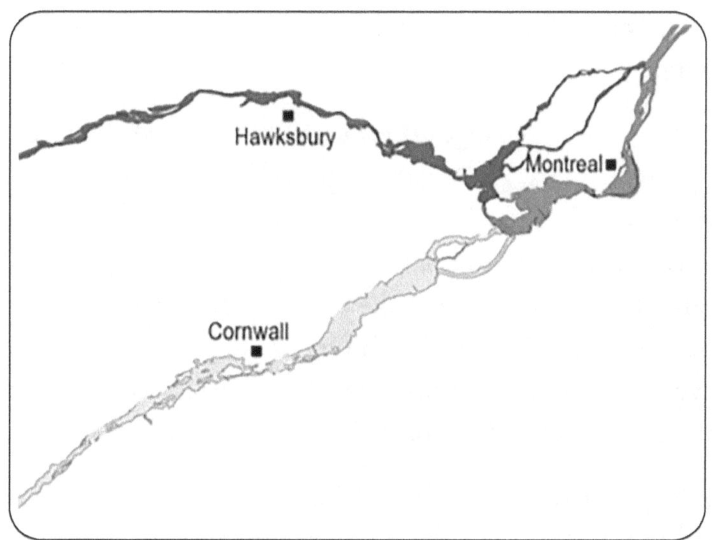


**St. Lawrence River**

One fine morning in the year 1981, soon after I reached US for my higher studies at the California State University, I received quite an unexpected call from my good old college friend Mr. Zachariah Jacob. Being busy in our own ways, we didn't have much interaction for a few years after graduation. When I took his call, I had no inkling that, it will pave the way for my rendezvous with River St. Lawrence.

We both had joined our engineering degree course in the year 1962, the year when the India – China war broke out. In those days, for an admission to the engineering course, in addition to securing the required marks in the qualifying examinations, one had also to give an undertaking to serve the defence forces, if called for. During that 5 year course, Mr. Zacharia Jacob was my hostel room-mate. By the time we completed our degree, the war was over, service in defence was no more mandatory, and we went our separate ways taking up jobs in civilian areas.

Today, after so many years, Zachariah called me from Toronto, Canada where he was working as a design engineer. He was living there with his family. Zachariah was calling me after hearing from our common friends about my arrival at California for my post-graduation in Environmental Engineering.

After the initial exchange of excuses on why one didn't contact the other for so many years, Zachariah suggested how we can make amends for that lapse. He was firm that, to begin with, I visit the Zachariahs forthwith. "Visiting us apart, you can see a lot of things of your interest here; like the Niagra Falls, Thousand Islands Lake etc", he lured me. Being a fresher in the University under a World Health Organisation Program, I was hesitant to get diverted. But, despite my best efforts, I couldn't shake off friend Zachariah, and I reached Canada within the next two weeks.

In hindsight, I was lucky that Mr. Zacharia coerced me to come over to Canada and go for a tour because, it gave me the chance to visit and get introduced to The St. Lawrence River, a river with lots of peculiarities right from its name, and the famous Thousand Islands Lake which too was unique in many ways.

We wasted no time in setting out on a site seeing spree. It was to the Thousand Islands Lake that we went first. The Thousand Islands constitute a North American Archipelago of 1864 islands that straddles the Canada – US border in the St. Lawrence River as it emerges from the North-east corner of Lake Ontario. Zachariah's cousin Lilly, who too was my friend, and Lilly's brother Lalan arranged the cruise ticket for us. The cruise ship was a huge luxury liner with many facilities to accommodate hundreds of people.

The Thousand Islands Lake is one of the largest sweet water lakes in the world. 60% of it is in US and 40% in Canada. Some of the islands in it are big, but many are small; some too small, of size just enough to hold the Bungalow in it. Most of these islands are privately owned by Hollywood celebrities. Many of them are with island mansions, Bungalows, resorts etc. This lake is famous as an Angler's paradise. The cruise in this massive lake was a wonderful experience.

The St. Lawrence river is a large river in the middle latitudes of North America, flowing from Lake Ontario in a roughly north-easterly direction into the Gulf of St. Lawrence, connecting the Great Lakes to the North Atlantic Ocean, and forming the primary drainage outflow of the Great Lakes Basin. The river traverses the Canadian provinces of Ontario and Quebec as well as the U.S. State of New York, and is part of the international boundary between Canada and the United States. It also provides the basis for the commercial St. Lawrence Seaway. The St. Lawrence River and Seaway are of vital geographic and economic importance to the Great Lakes system connecting the lakes to the Atlantic Ocean, and providing navigation to deep-draft ocean vessels.

The St, Lawrence River is 1200 kms long, and with a river basin of area 1344200 sq.km. This river is supposed to be the cleanest river in the US, and is ideal for swimming, fishing, boating, diving and other water sports. Montreal, Quebec City, Brockville, Cornwall etc are the cities on the banks of the St. Lawrence River.

St, Lawrence River, apart from its role as a major waterway of US at one time, finds mention in America's history also. In the year 1535, when it wasn't even 50 years after Columbus's arrival in America, Frenchman Jacus Cartier officially named this river as St. Lawrence, and claimed the stretch of land along the entire length of the river as belonging to France. That was the time when various European countries were staking claim for the ownership of the newly found land. But, in due course, the British got their control over America. With the establishment of Quebec City on the bank of St, Lawrence River by an administrator by name Samuel

Champlain in the 1600 – 1610 period, more and more people came over there to settle.

In the next century, in the series of wars fought during 1756 to 1763, it was the British who won. With that, the St, Lawrence River also came under British Control. But, before long, the American revolutionaries defeated Britain. Following this, this river became the boundary between the new republic and British Canada.

The river's tryst with history didn't end with that. In the battle of 1812, President James Madison sent an armada under General James Wilkinson to annexe Canada to America. On November 13, 1813, the General dropped anchor near the shore of Canada. In the war which ensued, the British and the Mohak warriors joined hands to defeat General James Wilkinson. With that, the control of St. Lawrence River came back to the British, and it became the trade corridor between the US Republic and Canada.

St. Lawrence Bay is the deepest estuary in the world. It is here in the Atlantic Ocean that the water from the massive lakes in North America coming through the St. Lawrence River falls. The average depth of this place is 148 metres. This bay is between the Labrador Peninsula and Quebec. Rivers Miramichi and Humber are the other rivers joining the St. Lawrence Bay. It is believed that till some 19000 years back, this whole region was covered with ice. Once the snow melted away, the topography and the biological diversity of the land was found to be ideal for fishing, encouraging the native fishermen folk to move over here.

It is now four decades since my chance visit to the Thousand Islands Lake which is among the prominent sweet water lakes in the world, and also to the historically important St. Lawrence River. Both were in pristine conditions at that time. However, they might have undergone a lot of changes during these four eventful decades when the world has witnessed mankind abusing the nature recklessly to further their vested interests. I can only hope that the lake and the river were spared from such onslaughts, and continue to retain their charm and beauty.

The memories of my time with the Thousand Islands Lake keep popping up occasionally. How can one forget the wavelets caressing the beautiful shores of those cute islands, and the sublime ambience they provide?

# THAMES

## River Basin Where History Bloomed

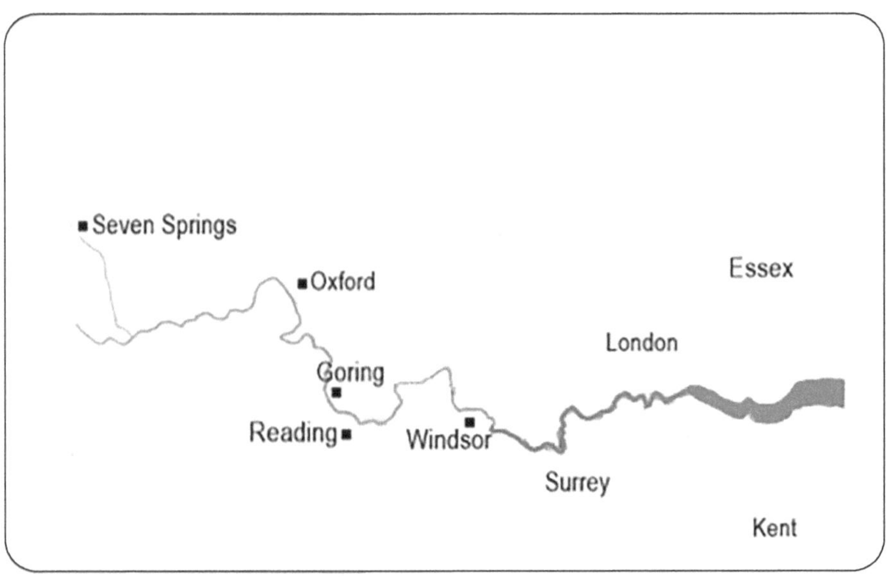

**Thames River**

Thames river flows through the heart of London, the city which housed the headquarters of the mighty British Empire which straddled most of the globe for centuries boasting as the only Kingdom where the sun never sets. Thames river is to the British, as River Ganga is to the Indians. Called River Isis in some parts of the country like Oxford, it is on the banks of this River Thames that the British culture evolved.

The origin of this river is from the snow-clad Cotswold Hill Ranges of south-central England as four small streams. It then flows some 350 km in the eastern direction to join the 29 km wide Thames Estuary in the North Sea. At 350 km, this river is smaller in length than most other rivers. But, if one considers the long list of historical events in which this river either participated or was witnessed, River Thames will be seen as validating the old saying 'size doesn't matter; it is all about your heart and your connections'.

The Thames is navigable by small boats up to the town bridge of Crick lade, close to the source, though motor cruisers and barges can go only till 16 km downstream. Flowing through lowlands, there are no waterfalls or rapids on the Thames. Rivers Lea, Leach, Churn, Coln, Windrush, Kennet, Evenlode, Cherwell and Ock are the major tributaries of the River Thames. The basin of this river is 14250 sq. km in size. London, Oxford, Reading and Windsor are the major cities on the banks of the Thames River. The authorities have prohibited all kinds of water sports and bathing in the river. This prohibition is in a view of the fact that nowadays, every year, some 20000 vessels pass through this river.

There was one Mr. Sridharan – we all call him Sridharetten – in London. He was a reputed Cost Accountant practising there. He was always there to lend a helping hand to especially Malayalees who happened to visit London in the 1960s and 70s, and needed some assistance. I had the opportunity to enjoy his hospitality at least a dozen times. He was the brother of my brother-in-law.

Often, as the Head of the Department of Environment and Safety with the Government of Dubai, I was required to visit some technical and scientific institutions in London. On all those trips, I ensured that a visit to Sridharetten was also in my itinerary. Later on, during my service as a Manager with the German company TUV Nord based at their Oman office, I used to drop in at Sridharettan's place and stay for a couple of days with him on my trips to Germany.

During the stays with Sridharettan, what I usually used to do was, get into Sridharettan's car as he leaves for his office, and get dropped somewhere near Hyde Park and roam there. As I go around looking at the London

Parliament, Buckingham Palace, the Thames River and the Kue Garden, memories of the stories I heard from my parents about the black days of British rule in India would come to my mind. This city was the capital of the British who, during their days of the occupation of India, crushed under their boots many of the civilian rights of the people there. The Regulating Act of 1773 to control and regulate the affairs of the East India Company in India; and also to recognise the political and administrative functions of the company, the Charter Act of 1813 legalising the colonisation of India for another 20 years etc were formalised here. The British viceroys Wellesley, Warren Hastings, Robert Clive, Dalhousie, Mount Batten etc who ruled India were doing so at the bidding of their masters sitting here.

This city played crucial roles in the world wars too. River Thames's involvement in wars dates back to AD 55 with the very first Roman military movement against England. But, the Roman dictator Julius Ceaser's forces couldn't conquer England. It was River Thames – referred to as Tamesis in Roman – which stood between the Romans and victory. But, one century later, another Roman Emperor by the name of Claudius crossed the Thames and conquered them.

During those days, the regions on either side of the River Thames were marshlands. It was the Roman army who built a bridge - a wooden one – for the first time across River Thames. They also constructed a port on the northern bank of the river and gave it the name Londinium. After that, this port started handling the freight movement between various parts of Europe.River Thames was used for the movement of goods from the interiors to this port. With that, Londinium became a leading business centre in Europe. It is this Londinyam which became London with time.

By the 4th century AD, Rome became weak, and its clout waned. Their span of control began to shrink. In due course, they had to leave Londinyam also. Consequently, River Thames and the port came to be neglected by all.

But after another 10 centuries, the city of London and the River Thames caught the attention of the world again. More and more businesses bloomed and prospered on the banks of the river. With that, the facilities in the river also got upgraded. In the year 1840, they drilled a 459 metres long tunnel under the river to connect the opposite banks of the river. That tunnel is still in use as a part of the Greater London Rail Subway.

There are 16 bridges on River Thames in the Greater London area alone. Most of them are road and rail bridges; but some, like the Golden Jubilee Bridges and the Millennium Bridge accommodate pedestrians. Tower Bridge, London Bridge, Millennium Bridge, Westminster Bridge, Waterloo Bridge etc are the major bridges in the Thames River. The Tower Bridge which is an attraction for tourists was completed in 1894. This bridge has provisions for raising two of its spans to facilitate the passage of ships underneath.

Till the construction of the Westminster Bridge in the middle of the 18th century, the only way to cross the Thames on foot was through the London Bridge. This was later reconstructed, and in the year 1820, a new bridge was built in its place. The 19 pillars which supported the London Bridge were offering big obstruction to the flow of water in the river. Because of that, it is said that, during the 600-odd years when the bridge was in use, at least on 8 occasions, the water in the river froze. There are also two-foot tunnels, one at Greenwich and the other at Woolwich, and several road and rail tunnels in this river.

The London Bridge in the heart of the city attracts travellers. It is very entertaining to watch the giant waves while standing enveloped in the cool breeze. Waves of up to 18 feet are not uncommon here. The urban Thames was once best admired from the deck of one of its many scheduled passenger boats. It can now also be viewed from the Millennium Bridge, the only bridge across the Thames that is solely for pedestrians, and from the London Eye, an enormous Ferris wheel.

Once, I and the present Head of the Department of Environment of the Dubai government visited the office of the Thames River Authority. The officers there explained to us the misfortunes of the river since the Second World War. The war had destroyed all the old Victorian drain lines and water treatment plants. In a way, that was like a biological warfare because as the river became polluted, that opened the floodgates for many contagious diseases. It took at least 20 years after the war to reconstruct them because the war had left the government penniless.

**Story of Pollution in River Thames. How a 'Biologically dead river was transformed into one of the world's cleanest rivers running through a city.**

Since at least the 10th century AD, River Thames became discernibly polluted from the ever-increasing number of people settling on its banks. The river was being used as a dumping yard for depositing waste materials of all kinds. In the absence of any kind of civic amenities for the disposal of sewerage in those days, rivers were the natural choice to take that burden.

Matters took a turn for the worse in the year 1858 when the stink from the river became so intolerable that people started vacating London. This was historically recorded as 'The Great Stink of 1858'. Following this, one civil engineer by name Sir Joseph Bazelgette was commissioned to build a sewage network to ease the problem, and his efforts helped to improve the condition. That was followed by over a century of improvements to the network, including upgrading sewage treatment facilities and installing household toilets linked to that system.

But, bombings across the city during the Second World War destroyed parts of that network allowing raw sewage to again enter the river. What's more, as the Thames widens and slows through central London, fine particles of sediment from its tributaries settled on the riverbed. These were contaminated with a range of heavy metals, creating a toxic aquatic environment.

Finally, the pollution in the river reached really dangerous levels. For most fish to thrive, the water they live in must contain at least 4-5 milligrams of dissolved oxygen per litre (mg/l). Measurements taken during the 1950s showed that dissolved oxygen (DO) levels in the Thames were only around 0.5 mg/l. It was even said that for the 20 miles of the Thames running through central London, the DO levels were too low – even not measurable. Validating these findings, in a 69 km length of the river from Kew to Gravesend, no fish was sighted in the 1950s. That meant, the river couldn't support most of the aquatic life. The worst was to follow. Surveys in 1957 confirmed the river was incapable of sustaining life, and the River Thames was eventually declared 'biologically dead' by the scientists at London's Natural History Museum.

That rang alarm bells at the right places and triggered a series of corrective measures. With considerable effort from policymakers, the river's fate began to change for the better. From 1976, all sewage entering the Thames was treated, and various legislations between 1961 and 1995 helped to raise the quality of water.

The privatisation of water companies by Prime Minister Margaret Thatcher also saw the establishment of the protective National Rivers Authority in 1989, as well as the introduction of biotic monitoring; both proving the much-needed impetus for anti-pollution activities.

Biotic monitoring is a scoring system that measures pollution by counting the macro-invertebrates such as mayflies, snails or water beetles in a river, and then giving each species a score according to its tolerance to low DO levels. Low overall scores meant that the river isn't capable of sustaining organisms needing oxygen to survive.

The river purification went beyond controlling the discharge of polluting substances into the river. One such idea was the installation of large oxygenators, or "bubblers", to increase the DO levels. In the early 1980s, the Thames Water Authority developed a prototype oxygenator mounted on a barge. Later, in 1988, a self-propelled "Thames Bubbler" was introduced, and yet another one in 1999. Together, they are responsible for maintaining oxygen in the river at a level sufficient to support the growing fish population.

As a result of all these initiatives, the water quality progressively improved, and fish started to return to the Thames River in the order of their DO requirement. Officially, the Flounder fish belonging to a group of fat fish species needing less oxygen, was the first fish variety to return to the Thames in 1967, followed by 19 freshwater varieties and 92 marine species such as the Bass and the Eel into the estuary and lower Thames. Finally, the return of the 'aristocratic' Salmons to the Thames in the 1980s was a thrilling marker for conservationists, to be followed by occasional sightings of even the oxygen-guzzling Seahorses.

Thus, from a 'biologically dead' stage, River Thames was resurrected to be acknowledged as one of the world's cleanest rivers running through a city. What is most remarkable about this is that the Thames made this extraordinary fairy-tale recovery in just 60 years after being declared "biologically dead" by the scientists at London's Natural History Museum. Another classic example of 'bringing the dead back from the grave'.

River Thames is a basic emotion in English life. Its banks were the venue of so many historical events which no other river in Europe can claim. Events like the drafting of the Magna Carta, the first document to put in writing the principle that the king and his government were not above law at Runnymede, a meadow of the river in 1215, the skies of England reverberating with the gunshots of wars, the starvation following the famine of the 15th century, the morbid days of plague when people dropped dead in thousands etc. Not to mention, Shelly, Keats, Milton, Wordsworth and the greatest of them all, Shakespeare enriching the English literature.

The Thames continues to flow carrying the good and bad memories of all these and much more.

# POTOMAC
## Reverberations of Revolutions

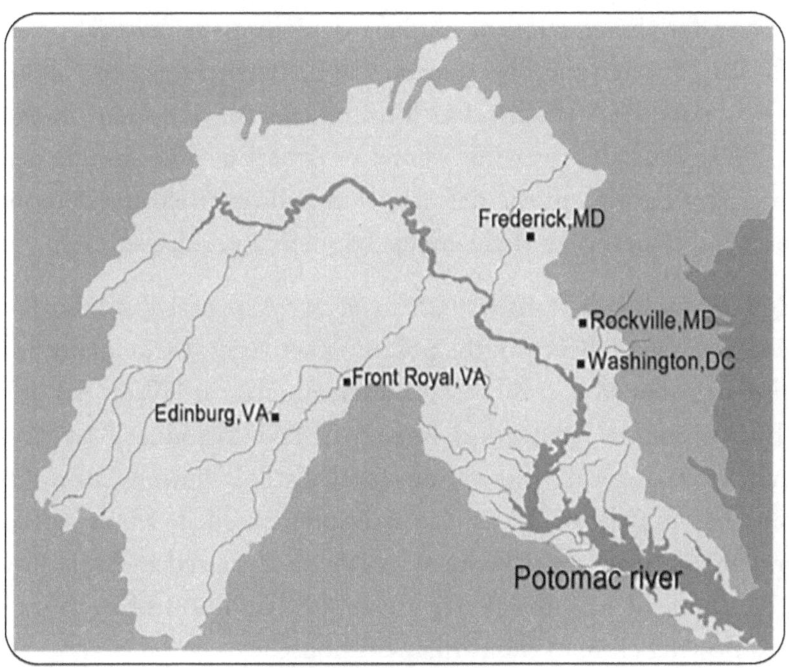

**Potomac River**

River Potomac is a small river passing through the States of Maryland, Pennsylvania, Virginia, West Virginia and Washington DC in America. Though, only some 640 km long, it is the fourth largest river along the East Coast of the US, and the 21st largest in the US. This river forms part of the borders between Maryland and Washington DC on the left descending bank and between West Virginia and Virginia on the right descending bank.

This river, originating from the Potomac Highlands and flowing into the Chesapeake Bay has nearly a dozen tributaries. Some 7 million people live in the basin of this river which is a favourite destination of tourists interested in water sports like angling, skiing, boating, riverside sightseeing etc. This river meets 90% of the water requirement of Washington DC.

The house and the estate of Mr. George Washington, the first President of the USA are on the bank of the Potomac River which was honoured by conferring the title the 'Heritage River of US' by President Bill Clinton in 1998. Sufficient funds were allotted for the beautification of the river banks, and for the creation of markers depicting the cultural heritage of the US. But, at one time, this river was so dirty with algae and all kinds of waste materials that, Mr. Lyndon Johnson, the US President in the years 1963 – '69 called the river the 'shame of America'. The mining activities near the river banks and the deforestation had hastened the deterioration of the river. Naturally, all these affected aquatic lives also severely.

However, with the famous 'Clean Water Act' of 1972', the Potomac River began to get relief from the polluting activities. Incidentally, it was in the same year that Mrs. Indira Gandhi introduced the 'Water Act' in India. The Environmental Protection Agency (EPA) introduced by President Nixon in 1970, together with various local Water Pollution Control Boards ensured that the Clean Water Act is implemented in all its seriousness. In comparison, even though the Water Act was passed in India way back in 1972, the least said the better about the condition of even the River Yamuna flowing close to the Parliament house.

River Potomac is home to a particular kind of shark known as the Bull Sharks growing up to lengths of up to 8 feet or even beyond. This is probably one reason why swimming in the river is prohibited. Another reason, of course, is the high level of pollution. However, thanks to decades of hard work following the Clean Water Act' of 1972, many indicators pointing to the improvement of Potomac's health are available now.

It was some 15 years back that I, accompanied by my wife, our daughter and her husband visited the Potomac River which was not far away from the campus of the College Park University of Maryland where we were staying. I remember, one day when we were lazily ambling on the bank of the river, the Police patrol who were on their rounds cautioned us thinking that we were preparing for a bath in the river.

There is a museum on the bank of the Potomac River. All the details of the Boston Tea Party of the year 1773 are inscribed on its walls. There, I could see some super senior US citizens going around reading those details seriously with various emotions flickering on their wrinkled faces. Perhaps, those inscriptions rekindled in them the memories of heroics of the American Revolution about which they might have heard from their parents.

# JORDAN

## Perseverance Is The Key For Survival

### Jordan River

We were flying to Aqaba in Jordan in an eight-seater executive jet for an official visit to a Phosphoric Acid Plant there. To reach our destination, the plane had to fly over the Red Sea, and later, the Jordan river. As we reached the Red Sea, the pilot lowered the plane, and gave us a lecture on the Red Sea, and the Jordan river. A while later, the plane was flying over River Jordan. We had included a visit to River Jordan, and some historically important places in that region in our itinerary.

River Jordan, called 'Nahr Al Sharieat' in Arabic, is a river in the Middle East. This river rises on the slopes of Mount Hermon, and flows roughly from north to south through the Sea of Galilee, and onto the Dead Sea. Jordan river flows through Israel, Jordan and Palestine. The city of Jericho is on its banks. At 251 km in length which is slightly longer than Kerala's Periyar river of only 244 km, this river is too small compared to the most of the rivers in the world. On the western side of the Jordan river is, the West Bank and Israel; and on the eastern side lies Jordan and the Golan Heights. It lies in a structural depression, and has the lowest elevation of any river in the world.

At the time of our visit, the whole region was tension-filled. Not surprising because, the parties involved here are Lebanon, Syria, Israel and the West Bank. So, our plans to visit the historic places there didn't work out.

River Jordan occupies an important place in Christianity and Judaism. The Bible speaks about the Israelites reaching their 'Promised Land' after crossing this river. It is believed that the river parted to facilitate the Israelites to cross over, but restored soon to drown their enemies who were in hot pursuit. Further, it is believed that it was in this river that John the Baptist baptised Jesus Christ. In a drama written by the late Mr. C.J. Thomas, River Jordan is symbolically presented while describing the romance between King David and Bathsheba, the mother of Solomon who succeeded David as the king.

River Jordan has nearly one dozen tributaries. Actually, in size, they are as small as the streams elsewhere. But, one shouldn't forget that these are in the desert. On either side of these 'rivers', one can see date palm fields, vegetable gardens and fruit cultivation. On these farms, there are nicely made small ponds with beautiful steps to go down. In the middle of some of these ponds, there is a mound where people can sit, similar to what we see in many of the temple ponds in Kerala.

The reduction in the flow rate of the Jordan river is a matter of huge environmental concern. Once upon a time, the flow rate of the river is 1.3 billion cu.m per year. But, it has reduced progressively to just 20 to 30 million cu.m in recent years with ominous portends. One can only pray for a turn around.

Coming to another environmental concern which is pollution, River Jordan has more than a fair share of this scourge. The first 3-kilometre below the Sea of Galilee, comprising a small section of the northernmost portion of the Lower Jordan, have been kept pristine for baptism and tourism. But, the 100-kilometre downstream stretch - a meandering stream from above the confluence with the Yarmulke, to the Dead Sea - is highly polluted. Environmentalists say, the practice of letting sewage, together with the flow of brackish water into the river has almost destroyed its ecosystem, and it could take decades to rescue the Jordan river. In 2007, Jordan river was named one of the world's 100 most endangered ecological sites.

To control the pollution in the River Jordan, the government of Jordan is receiving a lot of assistance from UNEP and the World Bank. But, sadly, due in part to the lack of cooperation between Israel and the neighbouring Arab States, nothing much has been achieved.

# SACRAMENTO
## The River With A Golden Touch

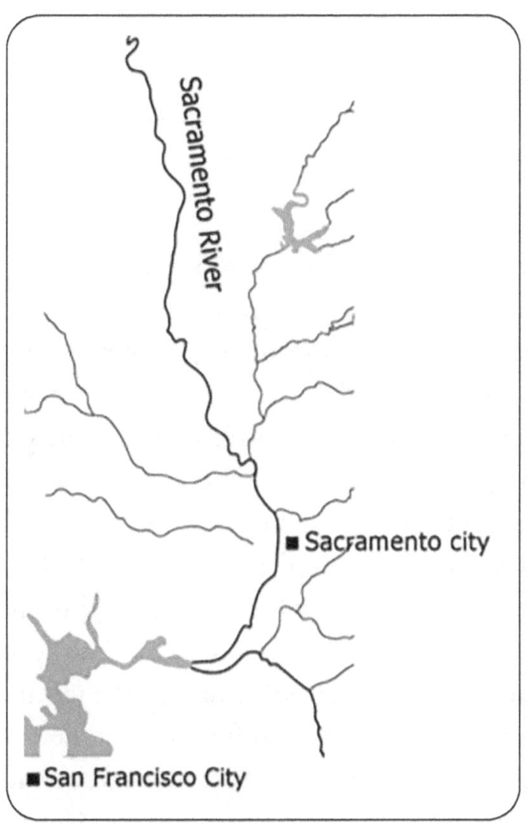


**Sacramento River**

Four decades back, I lived for a year in the United States in the town of Sacramento for my higher education there. The college where I studied at Sacramento was on the bank of the Sacramento River which was famous for fishing and transportation. Being away from family and friends, and in an entirely alien environment for the first time in my life, my early days there were stressful. The river close-by provided me with much needed solace in those days.

As far as I am concerned, there was nothing unusual about that. From my early teens, I had some affinity with rivers. Apart from that, till coming over to Sacramento, as the Regional Engineer of the Kerala State Pollution Control Board, Kozhikode, I was deeply involved in the antipollution drives in the rivers in Northern Kerala. With running feuds with the polluters – some of them industrial giants –, politicians and corrupt officials, my time there was eventful, to say the least. Maybe because of that also, in due course, rivers came to occupy an important place in my mind, and it didn't take too long for my attention to fall on the River Sacramento flowing so near.

So, ever since I arrived in Sacramento, I was itching for a visit to the Sacramento River. Fortunately for me, that opportunity came earlier than expected as part of my admission to the University. As was the custom there, the day previous to the starting day of the Fall Semester, the University organised a program to welcome the foreign students. Since our university was on the bank of the Sacramento river, it came in handy for the organisers to conduct this function in a beautiful garden situated between the Riverfront Centre and the Riverside Hall. On this occasion, the entire garden was decorated with colourful lights. Together with soft western music, it provided the perfect ambience. The beautiful hostesses of the function, running around attending to even the minutest detail added a tinge of glamour to the function. This function on the river bank provided me with the opportunity for my very first rendezvous with the river. After that, whenever I got time, I used to laze along the riverside.

The Sacramento River is the principal river of Northern California, and is the longest river in California. Rising in the Klamath Mountains, the river flows south for 400 miles before reaching the Sacramento–San Joaquin River delta and the San Francisco Bay. The principal tributaries of the Sacramento River are Pit, McCloud, Feather and American. River San Joaquin is another important river in California.

Farming is the mainstay of California's economy. As parts of the two irrigation projects viz. the Central Valley Project and the California State Water Project, they have built dams in most of the rivers in California to bolster agriculture. These projects reach the water from the water surplus northern California to the farms in the Central Valley and the areas of less water availability in Southern California. The shores, coasts, rivers, other water sources etc are under the control of the California Coastal Commission.

The water from the Sacramento River is used for farming in the Sacramento Valley. California is far ahead of many US states in wheat production. So too, when it comes to fruits and vegetables. They are exporting these products to the other States and countries. Branded 'California' apples are available in department stores in India also. Many households in California are using fruit juices in place of water as a drink to quench thirst because a litre of apple juice is only as expensive as half a litre of bottled water.

There were many vineyards and wineries also in this area. They are places of interest to university students. You are mistaken if you think, that is for the wrong reasons. The 'Fall Semester' in the college will end by the first week of December, and the next three weeks are vacation time. This coincides with the apple season, offering the opportunity for the students to earn some money by going for apple plucking. Many students will avail this opportunity to earn some pocket money for the Christmas – New Year bash. The novel 'The Grapes of Wrath' by the American writer John Steinbeck was based on the struggle of the people working in the vineyards of California.

California is a historically important State. Earlier, this was a part of Mexico. It got annexed by America after the battle of 1849, and on September 9, 1850, it became the 31st State of America. During the migration years, it was the Spanish people to arrive first in California. World-famous cities like Los Angeles and San Francisco are in the California State. Sacramento city on the banks of the Sacramento River is the capital of California State.

Water in the Sacramento River and its major tributaries is generally of good quality; the source being the melting snow collected in upstream reservoirs, and released in response to the water needs or flood control. The results of a study indicated that the number of dissolved solids in the Sacramento River and its major tributaries was low. But, at some locations, algae attached to streambed material was found abundant, which is usually related to higher-than-normal nutrient inputs to the streams. If this trends to increase, that can be a matter of concern because excess algae, apart from causing taste and odour problems in drinking water, could also lead to dissolved oxygen depletion, and thus affect aquatic life. Anyway, for now, no such effects were observed in the Sacramento River or its major tributaries.

Rivers support life. They soothe our minds. Whenever we find time to sit on a river bank and relax – whether it is the bank of a Californian river or our Chaliyar River back home -, we float in a sensation beyond the description of words. So, we should feel the pain whenever we see these rivers getting abused by fellow human beings. I am sure about one thing; my journey, holding rivers close to my heart, has been most fulfilling.

------------------------------------------------------------

# Tabulation of Salient features of Rivers

| River | Starting | Ending | States | Length | Tributaries | Cities | Countries |
|---|---|---|---|---|---|---|---|
| Ganges | Uttarakhand in the Himalayas Himadri In Gangotri glacier Gomukh | Bay of Bengal | Uttarakhand Uttar Pradesh Bihar Jharkhand Bengal | 2525KM | Ramganga, Gomati, Gagra, Gandak, Kosi, Yamuna, Son, Damodar | Rishikesh, Haridwar, Kanpur, Mirzapur, Varanasi, Patna, Bhagalpur,Calcutta | India, Bangladesh |
| Yamuna | Uttarakhand in the Himalayas Himadri Yamunotri | Allahabad (Prayagraj) | Uttarakhand, Haryana, Uttar Pradesh | 1376 km | Tons, Chambal, Sindh, Betwa, Ken | Delhi, Noida, Madura, Agra, Allahabad | India |
| Brahmaputra | Tibet in China Chemayung Dung Glacier | Bay of Bengal | Arunachal Pradesh, Assam | 2900 km (916-india) | Subansiri, Manas, Kemang, Teesta Dibang, Lohit, Dhansiri | Dibrugarh, Jorhat, Tezpur, Guwahati, | China, India, Bangladesh |
| Indus | Bogarju glacier in Tibet | Arabian Sea (Karachi) | Jammu and Kashmir, Ladakh | 3180 km (709-india) | Kabul,Chenab Ravi, Beas,Sutlej | Gilgit, Amritsar, Hyderabad, Karachi | Pakistan, India |
| Kaveri | Brahmagiri Hills of Karnataka (Cuttack District) | Bay of Bengal (Poombuhar) | Karnataka, Tamil Nadu | 800 km | Kabini, Bhavani Pambar,Amaravati | Talakaveri, Hassan, Krishna Raja Sagar, Mysore, Mettur, Eero, Thanjavu, Poompatnam | India |

| | | | | | | | |
|---|---|---|---|---|---|---|---|
| Krishna | Mahabaleshwar Hills of Maharashtra | Bay of Bengal | Maharashtra, Karnataka, Telangana, Andhra Pradesh | 1400 km | Bhima, Musi, Tungabhadra | Mahabaleshwar, Amaravati, Srisailam, Nagarjunakonda, Vijayawada | India |
| Mahanadi | Sihawa Hills of Chhattisgarh | Bay of Bengal | Chhattisgarh, Odisha | 858 km | Tel, Ib, Ong, Sheonath | Rajim, Sambalpur, Cuttack, Sonepur | India |
| Godavari | Trinity of Nashik, Maharashtra Bakeshwar | Bay of Bengal | Maharashtra, Odisha, Chhattisgarh, Andhra Pradesh | 1465 km | Indravati, Sabari Penganga | Trimbakeshwar, Nashik, Kopargaon, Paithan, Nanded, Rajahsmundry, Bhadrachalam | India |
| Narmada | Amaryantak Hills of Madhya Pradesh | Arabian Sea | Madhya Pradesh, Gujarat | 1312 km | Banjar, Hiran Tawa | Amarkantak, Jabalpur, Omkareshwar, Maheshwar, Vadodara, Dharampuri, Khandwa | India |
| Vaigai | Periyar Plateau Varumbanad Hills | Pak Strait | Tamil Nadu | 258 km | Suruliyar, Varaha Mullayar, Kottagudi Kiruthumal, Uppar | Theni, Dindigul, Madurai | India |
| Sabarmati | Aravalli in Rajasthan | Arabian Sea (Gulf of Khambhat) | Gujarat, Rajasthan | 371 km | Wakal, Harnav, Haramati Watrak | Udaipur, Ahmedabad, Gandhinagar | India |

| | | | | | | | |
|---|---|---|---|---|---|---|---|
| Potomac | Potomac Highlands | Chesapeake Bay | West Virginia, Maryland, District of Columbia | 652 km | • Left Conococheague Creek, Antietam Creek, Monocacy River, Rock Creek, Anacostia River • Right Kakapan River, Shenandoah River, Goose Creek, Occoquan River, Wicomico River | Cumberland, MD, Harpers Ferry, WV, Washington, D.C., Alexandria, VA | United States of America |
| St.Lawrence | Lake Ontario | Gulf of St. Lawrence | New York | 1197 km | Outaouais, Saguenay, Manicouagan, Saint-Maurice, Outardes Rivers | Quebec City, Montreal, Trois-Rivières, Cornwall, Brockvilles, Ogdensburg | Canada, United States of America |
| Rhine | The river originates in the Swiss canton of Graubünden in the southeastern Swiss Alps and forms part of the Swiss-Liechtenstein, Swiss-Austrian, Swiss-German, and then Franco-German borders, | Flowing in a northerly direction through the German Rhineland. The Netherlands eventually drains into the North Sea. | – | 1233 km | Thur, Toss, Glatt, Aare, Wutach from north | Cologne, Bingen, Mainz, Strasbourg, Ludwigshafen | Germany, France, Switzerland, Netherlands, Austria, Liechtenstein |

| Jordan | Anti-Lebanon mountain range of Mount Hermon in Golan Heights | Dead Sea, Jordan Rift Valley | - | 251 km | • Left Banias River, Dan River, Yarmouk River, Zarqa River • Right Hasbani or Snir River, Ion Stream | Jericho | Jordan, Israel, Palestine |
|---|---|---|---|---|---|---|---|
| Thames | Thames Head, near Kemble in the Cotswolds | North Sea | Wiltshire, Oxfordshire, Buckinghamshire, Surrey | 346 Km | Hurn, Leach, Cole, Cole, Windrush, Evenlode, Cherwell, Oak, Thame, Pang, Kennett,Loddon, Colne, Wey and Mole. | London, Henley-on-Thames, Oxford, Reading, Windsor | United Kingdom |

9 798888 836927